EDUCATION LIBRARY
UNIVERSITY OF KENTUCKY

New Directions for
Child and Adolescent
Development

Lene Arnett Jensen
Reed W. Larson
EDITORS-IN-CHIEF

William Damon
FOUNDING EDITOR

Digital Games: A Context for Cognitive Development

Fran C. Blumberg
Shalom M. Fisch
EDITORS

LIBRARY
UNIVERSITY OF KENTUCKY

Number 139 • Spring 2013
Jossey-Bass
San Francisco

Educ
LB
1029
.G3
D54
2013

DIGITAL GAMES: A CONTEXT FOR COGNITIVE DEVELOPMENT
Fran C. Blumberg, Shalom M. Fisch (eds.)
New Directions for Child and Adolescent Development, no. 139
Lene Arnett Jensen, Reed W. Larson, Editors-in-Chief

© 2013 Wiley Periodicals, Inc., A Wiley Company. All rights reserved.

No part of this publication may be reproduced, stored in a retrieval system, or transmitted in any form or by any means, electronic, mechanical, photocopying, recording, scanning, or otherwise, except as permitted under Sections 107 or 108 of the 1976 United States Copyright Act, without either the prior written permission of the Publisher or authorization through payment of the appropriate per-copy fee to the Copyright Clearance Center, 222 Rosewood Drive, Danvers, MA 01923; (978) 750-8400, fax (978) 646-8600. Requests to the Publisher for permission should be addressed to the Permissions Department, John Wiley & Sons, Inc., 111 River St., Hoboken, NJ 07030, (201) 748-6011, fax (201) 748-6008, www.wiley.com/go/permissions.

Microfilm copies of issues and articles are available in 16mm and 35mm, as well as microfiche in 105mm, through University Microfilms, Inc., 300 North Zeeb Road, Ann Arbor, Michigan 48106-1346.

ISSN 1520-3247   electronic ISSN 1534-8687

NEW DIRECTIONS FOR CHILD AND ADOLESCENT DEVELOPMENT is part of The Jossey-Bass Education Series and is published quarterly by Wiley Subscription Services, Inc., a Wiley company, at Jossey-Bass, One Montgomery Street, Suite 1200, San Francisco, CA 94104-4594. Periodicals postage paid at San Francisco, California, and at additional mailing offices. Postmaster: Send address changes to New Directions for Child and Adolescent Development, Jossey-Bass, One Montgomery Street, Suite 1200, San Francisco, CA 94104-4594.

New Directions for Child and Adolescent Development is indexed in Cambridge Scientific Abstracts (CSA/CIG), CHID: Combined Health Information Database (NIH), Contents Pages in Education (T&F), Educational Research Abstracts Online (T&F), Embase (Elsevier), ERIC Database (Education Resources Information Center), Index Medicus/ MEDLINE (NLM), Linguistics & Language Behavior Abstracts (CSA/ CIG), Psychological Abstracts/PsycINFO (APA), Social Services Abstracts (CSA/CIG), SocINDEX (EBSCO), and Sociological Abstracts (CSA/CIG).

INDIVIDUAL SUBSCRIPTION RATE (in USD): $89 per year US/Can/Mex, $113 rest of world; institutional subscription rate: $364 US, $404 Can/Mex, $438 rest of world. Single copy rate: $29. Electronic only–all regions: $89 individual, $364 institutional; Print & Electronic–US: $98 individual, $422 institutional; Print & Electronic–Canada/Mexico: $98 individual, $462 institutional; Print & Electronic–Rest of World: $122 individual, $496 institutional.

EDITORIAL CORRESPONDENCE should be e-mailed to the editors-in-chief: Lene Arnett Jensen (ljensen@clarku.edu) and Reed W. Larson (larsonr@ illinois.edu).

Jossey-Bass Web address: www.josseybass.com

CONTENTS

Blumberg, F. C., & Fisch, S. M. (2013). Introduction: Digital games as a context for cognitive development, learning, and developmental research. In F. C. Blumberg & S. M. Fisch (Eds.), *Digital Games: A Context for Cognitive Development. New Directions for Child and Adolescent Development, 139*, 1–9.

1

Introduction: Digital Games as a Context for Cognitive Development, Learning, and Developmental Research

Fran C. Blumberg, Shalom M. Fisch

Abstract

The authors present reasons why developmental psychologists should care about children's and adolescents' digital game play. These reasons may be identified as: a) digital game play is an integral aspect of children's and adolescents' lives; b) digital game play contributes to learning and cognitive development; and c) developmental research has the potential to contribute to effective educational game design. The authors expand on these reasons with the goal of introducing or reintroducing to developmental psychologists a rich and very relevant context in which to examine children's and adolescents' applied cognitive development. © 2013 Wiley Periodicals, Inc.

NEW DIRECTIONS FOR CHILD AND ADOLESCENT DEVELOPMENT, no. 139, Spring 2013 © Wiley Periodicals, Inc.
Published online in Wiley Online Library (wileyonlinelibrary.com). • DOI: 10.1002/cad.20026

1

W hy should developmental psychologists care about children's and adolescents' digital game play? This question motivated this volume and our 2012 Society for Research in Child Development symposium, on which many of the following chapters are based. As reflected in the chapters here, we argue that developmental psychologists should care, as digital game play provides a window into applied cognitive development and a continually expanding context in which children and adolescents spend their recreational and academic time. In fact, given greater movement toward the inclusion of digital games in academic settings (e.g., the Quest to Learn school in New York City), we further argue that developmental research can contribute to the design of effective educational games. We explicate our points below.

Digital Games Are an Integral Part of Children's Environments

On the broadest level, as developmental psychologists are interested in environmental influences on developmental trajectories, we must acknowledge that digital games have become an integral aspect of children's and adolescents' lives. For example, a 2009 Kaiser Family Foundation survey found that, on average, 8- to 18-year-olds spent approximately 90 minutes per day playing digital games (Rideout, Foehr, & Roberts, 2010). Findings internationally also point to extensive digital game play among children and adolescents in other developed countries, such as the United Kingdom and Germany (see Livingstone & Bober, 2005; Feierabend & Klingler, 2008). Given the increasing reach of cell phones and handheld devices as platforms for gaming, time spent playing digital games most likely has continued to rise. For example, recent findings indicate that most U.S. adolescents (58%) owned a smartphone (Nielsenwire, 2012) on which, on average, many may play about 15 hours of games per month (Carlozo, 2012).

The appeal of digital game play has been linked to several features, such as curiosity, challenge, and fantasy, as cited by Malone in his seminal 1981 article on the motivations for digital game play. More recently cited features that contribute to those noted by Malone include *interactivity*, which pertains to players' opportunity to initiate and receive feedback about their actions, which then influences the course of game play (Renkl & Atkinson, 2007; Ritterfeld, Shen, Wang, Nocera, & Wong, 2009); *agency* or *control*, which refers to players' ability to manage aspects of their game play, such as the use of the control mechanisms or flow of the story line (Wood, Griffiths, Chappell, & Davies, 2004; Qin, Rau, & Salvendy, 2009); *identity*, which refers to the player's opportunity to form relationships and linkages with characters within the game or become a game character via avatar construction (see Blascovich & Bailenson, 2011); *feedback*, which refers to the information players receive about the efficacy of their game actions and furthers interest in continuing game play via scaffolding of that play (Liao, Chen, Cheng, Chen, & Chan, 2011; Lieberman, 2006); and *immersion*, which refers to players' sense of presence or integration within the game (see Tamborini & Skalski, 2006). This feature, in particular, is often noted as the hallmark of digital games (Kickmeier-Rust & Albert, 2010) and has been linked to attainment of the highly pleasurable state of flow during game play (Csikszentmihalyi & Csikszentmihalyi, 1988; Sherry, 2004; Weber, Tamborini, Westcott-Baker, & Kantor, 2009). Collectively, these features contribute to engaging game experiences that promote sustained and repeated play.

Digital Games Contribute to Learning and Development

The persistent draw of digital game play and its clearly captivating nature has given rise to the development of academic/educational games and apps (See Deater-Deckard, Chang, & Evans, this volume) that capitalize on the features of recreational games (Moreno-Ger, Burgos, Martinez-Ortiz, Sierra, & Fernandez-Manjon, 2008), and to greater interest in exploring the cognitive benefits of digital game play (see Gee, 2003; Salonius-Pasternak & Gelfond, 2005; Squire, 2006). This interest, in turn, has contributed to the changing face of digital game research. For example, until fairly recently, the most widely known psychological research regarding digital game play concerned the potential negative impact of violent games (see Gentile, 2009; Gentile, Lynch, Linder, & Walsh, 2004; Weber, Ritterfeld, & Kostygina, 2006). However, evidence has been steadily accruing that attests to the positive ramifications of game play. For example, Bavelier, Green, and colleagues (Bavelier, Green, Pouget, & Schrater, 2012; Green & Bavelier, 2003; Green, Pouget, & Bavelier, 2010) have reported compelling evidence that frequent action digital game play promotes neural plasticity and cognitive abilities underlying one's ability to effectively learn in general. Indeed, under some conditions, even violent game play can carry benefits, although these benefits must be weighed against the risks of such play (Bavelier et al., 2012; Ferguson, 2010). For example, Ferguson and Garza (2011) recently demonstrated that adolescents who played more violent action games and had parents who were involved in their game play showed higher scores on a measure of civic attitudes and behaviors than their peers who played fewer such games and experienced less parental involvement in that play.

Data on the cognitive benefits of children's recreational play is consistent with findings linking video game play to enhanced reasoning and problem solving in older players and within educational games (e.g., Blumberg & Altschuler, 2011; Fisch, Lesh, Motoki, Crespo, & Melfi, 2011; Moreno, 2006; Schmidt & Vandewater, 2008). For example, research with college-age adolescents and adults has shown that playing digital games contributes to enhanced metacognition (VanDeventer & White, 2002), spatial reasoning (Green & Bavelier, 2006a, 2006b; Okagaki & Frensch,

New Directions for Child and Adolescent Development • DOI: 10.1002/cad

1994), and speed of processing (Dye, Green, & Bavelier, 2009). Fewer studies have been conducted with children or adolescents, as Blumberg and colleagues address in their chapter. However, the findings from this steadily expanding body of work suggest that the potential for analogous contributions to younger children's cognitive development also exists (e.g., De Lisi & Wolford, 2002; Papastergiou, 2009; Salonius-Pasternak & Gelfond, 2005).

Developmental Research Can Inform the Design of Better Educational Games

Decades of empirical research and practical experience have shown that developmental research and developmental researchers can play a vital role in the creation of educationally effective television series, such as *Sesame Street* (Fisch & Truglio, 2001; Sherry, in press). *Effective* in this context refers to viewers' ability to comprehend, acquire, and apply information gained via the screen. There are also ways in which developmental researchers can contribute to the design of effective educational digital games (see Revelle, this volume). Just as games can contribute to cognition and development, various aspects of cognition and development have an impact on children's interactions with games. For example, physical development has an impact on children's interaction with computer games, as mouse control is often difficult for young children who are still developing fine-motor coordination (Hourcade, Bederson, Druin, & Guimbretiere, 2004). Cognitive constraints, as reflected in attention (e.g., Calvert, 1999) and in working memory (e.g., Mayer & Johnson, 2010), also impact children's comprehension of onscreen material. Collectively, these findings have ramifications for the design of digital games to ensure age-appropriateness and usability for the age groups for which the games are intended.

Games as a Window into Applied Cognitive Development

Overall, digital games can be seen as a context for applied cognition. Specifically, these games are essentially cognitive puzzles (see Boyan & Sherry, 2011; Sherry, Lucas, Greenberg, & Lachlan, 2006) that encourage problem-solving approaches which are impacted by a wide range of developmental factors. In turn, they also present opportunities for players to practice and enhance cognitive skills. However, despite a substantial, emerging body of research examining the nexus of digital game play and children's and adolescents' cognitive skill enhancement, developmental psychologists are not the primary contributors to this literature. Similarly, too many educational games are developed for players of wide age ranges with little consideration of the differing levels of cognitive sophistication of those players (see Tüzün, 2007; Van Eck, 2006). To address these gaps, this volume explores children's and adolescents' interaction with digital games from the perspectives of both research and practice. Through reviews of the existing literature and newly emerging theoretical approaches, this volume highlights new work and thinking on the impact of digital game play on children's and adolescents' skills, development, and academic attainment, and ways in which principles of developmental psychology are applied to inform the creation of effective games.

Overview of the Volume

The volume opens with two chapters that review models regarding factors that contribute to the potential effectiveness of educational games.

Sherry's model draws on uses and gratifications theory as based in communication science, and findings from developmental science and cognitive science. According to Sherry, children's and adolescents' genre preferences and psychological needs hold ramifications for their engagement during educational game play. By taking these factors into account, educational game designers can create games that succeed in engaging children by matching the games with children's and adolescents' needs, goals, and game experience.

Deater-Deckard, Chang, and Evans' model focuses specifically on engagement states, seen as cognitive, behavioral, and affective in nature, and the relevance of these states to student learning during educational game play. As part of their discussion, the authors propose tools to measure engagement in the context of their newly developed educational game app to promote middle school students' algebra readiness.

Revelle provides an overview of the contributions of developmental theory and research to the design of effective educational games among preschool and elementary school–age players. For example, according to sociocultural views of developmental theory, learning is promoted via adult scaffolding of children's learning. As applied to educational games, established principles of scaffolding can be incorporated into the design of successive levels of difficulty within a game, and through the inclusion of developmentally appropriate hints and feedback that are triggered by a child's correct or incorrect response.

Blumberg, Altschuler, Almonte, and Mileaf survey the small but growing body of research concerning the cognitive benefits of digital game play among children and adolescents. They also review recent work detailing children's and adolescents' impression of the linkage between digital game play and school learning. Collectively, this research has ramifications for the development of effective educational games that engage their players and potentially promote the transfer of cognitive skills, strategies, and content attained and used during game play to more academic tasks.

Calvert, Staiano, and Bond provide an overview of the positive and negative impact of digital game play on the pressing problem of childhood obesity. Traditionally, digital game play has been seen as fostering sedentary behavior and as linked to consumption of high fat-, sugar-, and salt-based foods and beverages. However, Calvert and colleagues illustrate potential benefits of game play as reflected in the relatively recent genre of exergames for the promotion of physical activity and weight loss, and in mobile games and advergames for the promotion of healthy eating habits and practice.

The final chapter reaches beyond digital games, in keeping with current industry trends toward producing material that spans multiple media platforms, such as a related television series, digital game, hands-on activities, and even a live stage show. Fisch draws on several recent studies to explore the nature of *cross-platform learning* (i.e., learning from combined use of multiple media platforms) and how such learning compares to that of learning from a single medium. One key benefit appears to lie in transfer of learning, which allows the content learned from one medium to support richer learning from a second medium. This situation may be reflected in the acquiring of problem-solving strategies from a television series and the application of these strategies to the playing of an educational game in a more sophisticated fashion.

Levine and Vaala provide a closing commentary that examines key thrusts, governmentally and societally, in the push to use games as vehicles for informal and formal learning. They also highlight cross-cutting themes across the chapters, such as the role of student engagement in learning, the need to consider the developmental appropriateness of games designed for child and adolescent audiences, and their ramifications for advancing research and development concerning games as a vehicle for educational enhancement.

As these chapters illustrate, there are many substantive answers to the question, "Why should developmental researchers care about children's and adolescents' digital game play?" Such games have become an integral part of many children's and adolescents' environments, and they can be used to promote learning and development. We hope this volume will open this emerging body of research to the attention of a broader audience of developmental researchers, demonstrate the potential of games as a context for applied developmental research, and stimulate further theory and research to advance the field. Digital games may be "child's play"—but they are a form of "child's play" that is certainly worthy of substantive study.

References

Bavelier, D., Green, C. S., Pouget, A., & Schrater, P. (2012). Brain plasticity through the lifespan: Learning to learn and action video games. *Annual Review of Neuroscience*, 35, 391–416.

Blascovich, J., & Bailenson, J. (2011). *Infinite reality: Avatars, eternal life, new worlds, and the dawn of the virtual revolution*. New York, NY: HarperCollins.

Blumberg, F. C., & Altschuler, E. A. (2011). From the playroom to the classroom: Children's views of video game play and academic learning. *Child Development Perspectives, 5*, 93–103.

Boyan, A., & Sherry, J. L. (2011). The challenge in creating games for education: Aligning mental models with game models. *Child Development Perspectives, 5*, 82–87.

Calvert, S. L. (1999). The form of thought. In I. E. Sigel (Ed.), *Development of mental representation* (pp. 453–470). Mahwah, NJ: Lawrence Erlbaum Associates.

Carlozo, L. (2012, July 26). Interest compounds in finance game apps. *Reuters*. Retrieved from www.reuters.com/article/2012/07/26/us-financial-literacy-games-idUSBRE86P0ZQ20120726

Csikszentmihalyi, M., & Csikszentmihalyi, I. S. (1988). *Optimal experience: Psychological studies of flow in consciousness*. Cambridge, England: Cambridge University Press.

De Lisi, R., & Wolford, J. L. (2002). Improving children's mental rotation accuracy with computer game playing. *The Journal of Genetic Psychology, 163*, 272–282.

Dye, M. W., Green, C. S., & Bavelier, D. (2009). Increasing speed of processing with action video games. *Current Directions in Psychological Science, 18*, 321–326.

Feierabend, S., & Klingler, W. (2008). Was Kinder sehen. Eine Analyse der Fernsehnutzung 3- bis 13-Jähriger. *Media Perspektiven, 4*, 190–204.

Ferguson, C. J. (2010). Blazing angels or resident evil? Can violent video games be a force for good? *Review of General Psychology, 14*, 68–81.

Ferguson, C. J., & Garza, A. (2011). Call of (civic) duty: Action games and civic behavior in a large sample of youth. *Computers in Human Behavior, 27*, 770–775.

Fisch, S. M., Lesh, R., Motoki, E., Crespo, S., & Melfi, V. (2011). Children's mathematical reasoning in online games: Can data mining reveal strategic thinking? *Child Development Perspectives, 2*, 88–92.

Fisch, S. M., & Truglio, R. T. (Eds.). (2001). *"G" is for growing: Thirty years of research on children and Sesame Street*. Mahwah, NJ: Lawrence Erlbaum.

Gee, J. P. (2003). *What video games have to teach us about learning and literacy*. New York, NY: Palgrave Macmillan.

Gentile, D. A. (2009). Pathological video-game use among youth ages 8 to 18. A national study. *Psychological Science, 20*, 594–602.

Gentile, D. A., Lynch, P. J., Linder, J. R., & Walsh, D. A. (2004). The effects of violent video game habits on adolescent hostility, aggressive behaviors, and school performance. *Journal of Adolescence, 27*, 5–22.

Green, C. S., & Bavelier, D. (2003). Action video game modifies visual selective attention. *Nature, 423*(6939), 534–538.

Green, C. S., & Bavelier, D. (2006a). Effect of action video games on spatial distribution of visuospatial attention. *Journal of Experimental Psychology: Human Perception and Performance, 32*, 1465–1478.

Green, C. S., & Bavelier, D. (2006b). Enumeration versus multiple object tracking: The case of action video game players. *Cognition, 101*, 217–245.

Green, C. S., Pouget, A., & Bavelier, D. (2010). Improved probabilistic inference, as a general learning mechanism with action video games. *Current Biology, 20*, 1573–1579.

Hourcade, J. P., Bederson, B., Druin, A., & Guimbretiere, F. (2004). Differences in pointing task performance between preschool children and adults using mice. *ACM Transactions on Computer Human Interaction, 11*(4), 357–386.

Kickmeier-Rust, M. D., & Albert, D. (2010). Micro-adaptivity: Protecting immersion in didactically adaptive digital educational games. *Journal of Computer Assisted Learning, 26*, 95–105.

Liao, C. C., Chen, Z.-H., Cheng, H. N., Chen, F.-C., & Chan, T.-W. (2011). My-Mini-Pet: A handheld pet-nurturing game to engage students in arithmetic practices. *Journal of Computer Assisted Learning, 27*, 76–89.

Lieberman, D. A. (2006). What can we learn from playing interactive games? In P. Vorderer & J. Bryant (Eds.), *Playing video games. Motives, responses, and consequences* (pp. 379–397). Hillsdale, NJ: Lawrence Erlbaum Associates.

Livingstone, S., & Bober, M. (2005). *UK children go online*. Swindon, England: ESRC. Retrieved from www.lse.ac.uk/collections/children-go-online/UKCGO_Final_report .pdf

Malone, T. W. (1981). Toward a theory of intrinsically motivating instruction. *Cognitive Science, 4*, 333–369.

Mayer, R. E., & Johnson, C. I. (2010). Adding instructional features that promote learning in a game-like environment. *Journal of Educational Computing Research, 42*, 241–265.

Moreno, R. (2006). Learning in high-tech and multimedia environments. *Current Directions in Psychological Science, 15*, 63–67.

Moreno-Ger, P., Burgos, D., Martinez-Ortiz, I., Sierra, J. L., & Fernandez-Manjon, B. (2008). Educational game design for online education. *Computers in Human Behavior, 24*, 2530–2540.

Nielsenwire. (2012, September 16). Young adults and teens lead growth among smartphone owners. *Nielsenwire*. Retrieved September 14, 2012, from http://blog.nielsen .com/nielsenwire/online_mobile/young-adults-and-teens-lead-growth-among -smartphone-owners/

Okagaki, L., & Frensch, P. (1994). Effects of video game playing on measures of spatial performance: Gender effects in late adolescence. *Journal of Applied Developmental Psychology, 15*, 33–58. doi:10.1016/0193-3973(94)90005-1

Papastergiou, M. (2009). Digital Game-Based Learning in high school Computer Science education: Impact on educational effectiveness and student motivation. *Computers & Education, 52*, 1–12. doi:10.1016/j.compedu.2008.06.004

Qin, H., Rau, P. L., & Salvendy, G. (2009). Measuring player immersion in the computer game narrative. *International Journal of Human-Computer Interaction, 25*, 107–133.

Renkl, A., & Atkinson, R. K. (2007). Interactive learning environments: Contemporary issues and trends. An introduction to the special issue. *Educational Psychology Review, 19*, 235–238.

Rideout, V. J., Foehr, U. G., & Roberts, D. F. (2010). *Generation M²: Media in the lives of 8–18 year-olds*. Menlo Park, CA: Kaiser Family Foundation.

Ritterfeld, U., Shen, C., Wang, H., Nocera, L., & Wong, W. L. (2009). Multimodality and interactivity: Connecting properties of serious games with educational outcomes. *Cyberpsychology & Behavior, 12*, 691–697.

Salonius-Pasternak, D. E., & Gelfond, H. S. (2005). The next level of research on electronic play: Potential benefits and contextual influences for children and adolescents. *Human Technology: An Interdisciplinary Journal on Humans in ICT Environments, 1*, 5–22.

Schmidt, M. E., & Vandewater, E. A. (2008). Media and attention, cognition, and school achievement. *Children and the Electronic Media, 18*, 63–85.

Sherry, J. L. (2004). Flow and media enjoyment. *Communication Theory, 14*, 328–347.

Sherry, J. L. (in press). Formative research for STEM educational games: Lessons from the *Children's Television Workshop. Zeitschrift für Psychologie, 2*.

Sherry, J. L., Lucas, K., Greenberg, B. S., & Lachlan, K. (2006). Video game uses and gratifications as predictors of use and game preferences. In P. Vorderer & J. Bryant (Eds.), *Playing video games: Motives, responses, consequences* (pp. 213–224). Mahwah, NJ: Lawrence Erlbaum.

Squire, K. (2006). From content to context: Videogames as designed experience. *Educational Researcher, 35*, 19–29.

Tamborini, R., & Skalski, P. (2006). The role of presence in the experience of electronic games. In P. Vorderer & J. Bryant (Eds.), *Playing video games. Motives, responses, and consequences* (pp. 225–240). Hillsdale, NJ: Lawrence Erlbaum Associates.

Tüzün, H. (2007). Blending video games with learning: Issues and challenges with classroom implementations in the Turkish context. *British Journal of Educational Technology, 38*, 465–477.

VanDeventer, S. S., & White, J. A. (2002). Expert behavior in children's video game play. *Simulation and Gaming, 33*, 28–48. doi:10.1177/1046878102033001002

Van Eck, R. V. (2006). Digital game-based learning. *Educause Review, 41*(2), 17–30.

Weber, R., Ritterfeld, U., & Kostygina, A. (2006). Aggression and violence as effects of playing violent video games? In P. Vorderer & J. Bryant (Eds.), *Playing video games: Motives, responses, and consequences* (pp. 347–361). Mahwah, NJ: Lawrence Erlbaum Associates.

Weber, R., Tamborini, R., Westcott-Baker, A., & Kantor, B. (2009). Theorizing flow and media enjoyment as cognitive synchronization of attentional and reward networks. *Communication Theory, 19*, 397–422.

Wood, R., Griffiths, M. D., Chappell, D., & Davies, M. (2004). The structural characteristics of video games: A psycho-structural analysis. *CyberPsychology & Behavior, 7*, 1–10.

FRAN C. BLUMBERG is an associate professor in the Division of Psychological & Educational Services, Fordham University Graduate School of Education, New York, USA. Blumberg's research concerns the study of children's and adolescents' learning in the context of media-based settings. She has secured funding for this work from the Spencer Foundation and in 2010 convened a National Science Foundation–sponsored conference, Academic Lessons from Video Game Learning, *to develop a focused research agenda to study the ramifications of digital games for children's and adolescents' STEM learning. She can be reached via e-mail at blumberg@fordham.edu.*

SHALOM M. FISCH is president and founder of MediaKidz Research & Consulting, New Jersey, USA. As president and founder of MediaKidz Research & Consulting, Shalom Fisch applies developmental research and educational practice to inform the creation of effective educational media for children in the United States and around the world. He literally "wrote the book" on children's learning from media—twice—through his two books, "G" Is for Growing: Thirty Years of Research on Children and Sesame Street *(co-edited with Rosemarie Truglio) and* Children's Learning from Educational Television: Sesame Street and Beyond. *He can be reached via e-mail at mediakidz@lycos.com.*

Sherry, J. L. (2013). The challenge of audience reception: A developmental model for educational game engagement. In F. C. Blumberg & S. M. Fisch (Eds.), *Digital Games: A Context for Cognitive Development. New Directions for Child and Adolescent Development, 139,* 11–20.

2

The Challenge of Audience Reception: A Developmental Model for Educational Game Engagement

John L. Sherry

Abstract

According to educational gaming advocates, the engaging nature of games encourages sustained game play and enhanced attention to learning outcomes among players. Because children's and adolescents' play time varies by game genre, engagement with a game likely reflects the match between the genre and the player's preferences and needs. Youth learn which games are likely to promote satisfying psychological needs and yield positive experiences, which then informs their engagement with the games. A model is presented for research and development of educational games based on uses and gratifications theory from communication science, as well as developmental science and cognitive science findings. © 2013 Wiley Periodicals, Inc.

Scholars are increasingly advocating the use of video and computer games for education (Aldrich, 2004; Gee, 2007; Mishra & Foster, 2007; Ritterfeld, Cody, & Vorderer, 2010). An extension of the widely used *entertainment-education* strategy (Salmon, 2000; Singhal & Rogers, 1999; Singhal, Cody, Rogers, & Sabido, 2004), it is believed that the entertaining properties of games can be leveraged to engage students while they learn less-than-engaging material. There is every reason to believe that this relatively new and highly popular mass medium could make a powerful platform for education (Gee, 2007; Prensky, 2000). In addition to commanding tremendous amounts of player attention and time, games can be tailored to individual ability levels, facilitate individual study through repetition or discovery, and simulate just about any phenomenon a teacher might want students to understand (Sherry & Pacheco, 2006). In fact, computer games can be used to demonstrate processes that are not otherwise possible in a classroom (e.g., simulating a billion years of geophysical development).

Research and advocacy have accompanied a plethora of attempts to create educational games; in one recent content study, Ratan and Ritterfeld (2010) identified more than 600 such games for analysis. Despite the tens of millions of dollars that have been poured into the pursuit of educational computer games by governments and foundations, it is difficult to identify one outstanding example of an educational game that is broadly used and shown to be effective, like television's *Sesame Street*. Why is this the case? There are several possibilities. Perhaps the optimistic speculation is simply wrong and children cannot learn from games. More likely, the main problem is that the efforts to date have largely ignored the type of scientific evidence that Children's Television Workshop (CTW) producers used to create so many successful television shows. Multiple literature reviews have identified a dearth of research on how learners interact with the formal features of games, such as game avatars, speed, outcome goal (e.g., chase, construct, race, explore; Blumberg & Ismailer, 2009; Hays, 2005; Mitchell & Savill-Smith, 2004; Sherry & Dibble, 2009). One important factor that has been neglected in the research is the effect of development on game play and the motivations for game play. In this article, we consider the large literature on media use and on child development to point toward research areas that still need attention.

Media Reception Processes

Advocates argue that the engaging nature of the games will lead players to spend more time and think more deeply about the learning outcomes while playing these games. This approach, broadly referred to as *entertainment-education* (EE), has been used around the world for years with a wide range of media in an effort to make didactic educational and development messages (e.g., better farming practices, limiting family size, condom use.)

NEW DIRECTIONS FOR CHILD AND ADOLESCENT DEVELOPMENT • DOI: 10.1002/cad

more palatable for audiences (see Singhal & Rogers, 1999). Unfortunately, the EE approach has not shown straightforward evidence of success; sometimes audiences even show signs of resistance to these messages (Sherry, 1997). Often, as is the case with educational games, EE messages compete for attention with a number of other media messages, many of which are produced with large budgets solely for entertainment (Sherry, 2002). In general, children believe that educational games pale in comparison to the production quality of commercial games (Mitchell & Savill-Smith, 2004).

The EE approach takes an effects perspective, focusing on what the message will do to a passive media user without accounting for motivations, competition, and other factors in the reception process. It is not surprising that the effects approach has not yielded evidence of robust effects. The small effect sizes found in much media effects research (generally around 3–4% variance explained) suggest that there isn't a simple linear relationship between message exposure and effects. If psychologists are unable to find evidence of strong effects in highly controlled experiments with very sensitive measures, why would we expect a strong effect amid the clutter of real life?

The uses and gratifications perspective, from communication science, argues that individuals use media for a variety of purposes in response to the challenges found in their life ecology (Ruggiero, 2000). Uses and gratifications (U&G) represents one of the oldest and largest traditions of media research. Unlike effects research, U&G posits an active individual who purposefully uses media to satisfy perceived needs and solve problems. Media use represents an individual's choice to learn information, increase or decrease arousal, spend time with friends, and many other uses. According to Rosengren's (1974) U&G model, the interaction of basic human needs, individual differences, and social factors leads to perceived problems or deficits (e.g., lack of knowledge, need for competition, diminished arousal), for which media use may be one solution. Over time, individuals learn which media content is effective in addressing the various problems encountered. Because people control their own exposure to media and the motivations for that exposure, the effects of media are a function of the purpose for that use. For example, an individual may read a newspaper to find out the latest sports scores; knowledge of the score is the media effect. There is a key implication here for educational games; mere exposure doesn't cause strong effects, but purposeful use does. Playing a game with the purpose of learning will result in greater educational effects than playing the same game for fun. Our growing understanding of underlying neural mechanisms confirm this assertion. According to Lisman and Grace (2005), information is assigned to long-term memory storage if it meets the dual criteria of motivational importance and novelty. Therefore, dressing educational material in an entertaining game format is not sufficient to cause learning without concurrent motivation to store information in long-term memory. Ultimately, the game player chooses what and when to learn.

What motivates children to play computer games? A number of studies have looked at the reasons children give for game use. Olson (2010) reviewed the literature on game play motivations and categorized them into three groups: 1) social motivations, 2) emotional motivations, and 3) intellectual/expressive motivations. Social motivations encompass a variety of purposes, including competing with others, hanging out with friends, making friends, and opportunities for leadership or for teaching others. Emotional motivations include playing games to manage mood (e.g., arousal/excitement) and the opportunity to experience the intrinsically rewarding, highly focused state called *flow* (see Csikszentmihalyi, 1988; Sherry, 2004). Finally, Olson found a variety of intellectual motivations, including playing for the challenge, experiencing creativity, experimenting with different identities, and curiosity/discovery. She also surveyed 12- to 14-year-olds and found that five of the 17 motivations were endorsed by at least 40% of subjects: fun (70%), excitement (40%), reduction of boredom (48%), challenge of figuring something out (45%), and competition with others to win (40%). Sherry, Lucas, Greenberg, and Lachlan (2006) identified a similar set of motivations and tested them with a sample of children ranging from 10 to 18 years of age. These reasons included the challenge of beating the game, competition against friends and others, fantasy of doing something one cannot do in real life, diversion from problems, excitement/arousal, and a way of interacting socially (Sherry, Lucas, et al., 2006). The importance of these motivations varied across ages, with the 10-year-olds primarily playing for challenge and arousal, 13-year-olds enjoying competition with friends; and 16-year-olds playing primarily for competition and diversion. Further, the motivations varied within each age group by sex, with boys reporting higher levels of most motivations. However, regression analysis showed that social interaction was the main reason girls played games, while boys tended to play for arousal.

It is unsurprising that motivations for game play vary across age groups. Consistent with U&G, the degree to which individuals experience emotional, social, and intellectual motivations should change as emotional, social, and intellectual needs change developmentally. Thus, U&G is consistent with the life span developmental maxim that children both produce and are produced by their environment (Bronfenbrenner, 2005; Lerner, 1978, 1982; Scarr & McCartney, 1983). For example, in the study by Sherry, Lucas, and colleagues (2006), there was a clear shift from playing alone to playing with a friend for competition as developmental demands and opportunities for socialization change. Consistent with more general developmental patterns (Hartup & Stevens, 1999), older children (early and mid teens) were more likely to cite the social motivation of playing for competition with friends than were younger children (middle childhood), and social motivations accounted for more variance in game play time for older children.

As subtle and dramatic shifts in development create new perceived problems for children, motivations for game play should change, along with particular preferred game genres. For example, Greenberg, Sherry, Lachlan, Lucas, and Holmstrom (2010) found that individuals who were higher on social motivations to play such as competition and social interaction were more likely to prefer game genres that permitted social interaction, such as racing or sports games. This is consistent with general case, in which early teens engage in less social interaction than older teens. Similarly, games that require a higher level of cognitive development, such as strategy games, were more likely to appeal to older children than younger children, consistent with Hale's (1990) finding that cognitive processing skills needed to solve game challenges vary by age.

If we want children to be engaged with educational games, we need to consider what it is that brings them to the game play environment and what they expect from the experience. U&G provides a valuable window into patterns of game genre preference across developmental stages. As such, game engagement is facilitated when the right type of game is chosen for the changing developmental needs of the target audience. Considerations include developmental abilities/demands, game play motivations, and game genre attributes. Figure 2.1 provides a system for thinking through game learning.

Developmental Factors. The first considerations are the developmental demands and the developmental abilities of the learners. As human systems theorists (Bronfenbrenner, 2005; Lerner, 1978), cognitive scientists (e.g., Tomasello, Carpenter, Call, Behne, & Moll, 2005), social learning theorists (e.g., Bandura, 1986), and situative learning theorists (Derry & Steinkuehler, 2003) argue, learning occurs in a social context. The social context can provide structure, encouragement, behavioral models, and support to varying degrees as the individual progresses through the lifespan. According to U&G, the social context is an important source for motivations to use media.

We can imagine a broad array of developmental changes that could affect engagement with educational games. Social motivations would change as children shift from near-exclusive family influence to peer

Figure 2.1. Model for Game Engagement

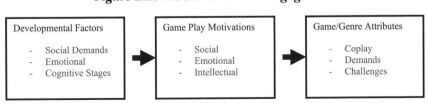

influence in the teen years. These changes would be realized in greater desire for computer games that allow coplay, as well as a desire to keep up with the latest popular games as a form of social bonding. For young children, the main social context is the family. Hence, parents can exert more influence on young children to use educational games by providing more educational than recreational games, coplaying, or even requiring a certain amount of learning time per day. As peer influence increases, motivations to play games that others are playing come to the forefront. The importance placed on learning within a peer group can also effect whether educational games are acceptable. Opportunities for peer activities such as clubs or sports can take away from time available to play educational games. Additionally, peer play carries implications of competition, including encouragement to perform at the highest levels as well as potential loss of interest in gaming due to poor performance relative to peers (Sherry, Lucas, et al., 2006; Vorderer, Hartmann, & Klimmt, 2003; Schmierbach, Xu, Oeldorf-Hirsch, & Dardis, 2012).

Emotional motivations would likely be effected by mood changes initiated by hormonal changes during puberty. At the extremes, the interaction between frequent and intense negative mood states during puberty and the highly satisfying experience of flow (Sherry, 2004) during game play could result in escapist patterns of play resembling addiction. Intellectual motivations, accompanied by developmental advancements in cognitive abilities, would drive a shift in genre preference from simple children's games to games that present more complex intellectual challenges such as simulations and strategy games. Additionally, individual differences in cognitive skills such as three-dimensional mental rotation, targeting, or object location memory can be instrumental in leading children to some games and away from others.

Game Play Motivations. As the social context shifts relative to developmental trajectories, motivations for educational game play also change. Shifts in genre preference due to the interaction between cognitive skills and intellectual motivations, such that gamers should prefer more demanding games as they develop cognitively, are predicted by U&G. Several studies have shown a strong correlation between genre preference and level of ability in a number of cognitive skills. In an experimental study with college students, Sherry, Rosaen, Bowman, and Huh (2006) showed that success at game play was a function of cognitive skills such as three-dimensional mental rotation, verbal fluency, targeting, and object location memory, and that success at the game was strongly correlated with liking and intention to play again. Boot, Kramer, Simons, Fabiani, and Gratton (2008) found that expert gamers outperformed non-gamers on a variety of cognitive skills, including object tracking, change detection, task switching, and mental rotation. After allowing the non-gamers 21.5 hours of practice playing a first-person shooter, the differences remained, suggesting that either gamers were naturally superior at these skills or that 21 hours was not adequate to offset the gains experienced from long-term playing. However, focus groups with both gamers and non-gamers suggest that the former is a strong possibility (Sherry, Lucas, et al., 2006). Non-gamers frequently cited poor performance in comparison to friends as a reason they stopped playing games. Additionally, non-gamers also stated that they found three-dimensional interfaces confusing and disorienting, suggesting that deficits in three-dimensional mental rotation were deterrents to game play.

Other motivations may include the desire to play games to maintain relationships (e.g., via coplaying with peer groups) and one's place in the relationship (e.g., via knowledge of popular games). Additionally, the notion of challenge as an intellectual motivation may differ across individuals. For example, Sherry, Lucas, and colleagues (2006) found that individuals with task-persistent temperament (e.g., the length of time children continue an activity despite obstacles) were more likely to play complex simulation games, while individuals who were low on task persistent temperament were more likely to play the less challenging kids games.

Game/Genre Attributes. Just as there are diverse needs, there are diverse game genres to serve those needs (Sherry & Pacheco, 2006). Thus, genres provide a broad palate of play options that can accommodate different developmental needs, individual differences, and game play motivations. Various game genres may emphasize highly graphic and complex environments (e.g., shooters), simple clear objectives and patterns (e.g., puzzle games), extensive puzzle solving (e.g., strategy, fantasy role playing), exploration (simulations), or greater social interaction (online games; Spence & Feng, 2010). Over time, children learn which game genres are useful for satisfying their emerging and changing psychological needs. Thus, they approach each genre with a set of expectations such that interest in game genre varies by age (Greenberg et al., 2010). Therefore, it is likely that some genres would better engage learners' attention at different times in the lifespan, relative to their perceived needs.

Discussion

A fundamental finding of the extensive U&G literature has been that individuals are selective in their media choices and that these choice are a function of desired solutions to perceived problems (Ruggiero, 2000). Developmental science provides the context and understanding of how both abilities and demands change across the lifespan. Finally, cognitive science tells us that assigning information to long-term memory and organizing information in long-term memory are functions of the individuals' experiences and motivations to remember particular information. Taken as a whole, the lesson painted is of a motivated, active learner finding, perceiving, and storing information.

Why did *Sesame Street* work so well? The CTW understood that preschool children were self-motivated to learn about the world and the symbol systems that older family members use. They also understood from U&G research that children primarily used television for learning. The developmental goal and the medium were an excellent match. CTW also understood that parental approval was a strong motivator for preschoolers, so they encouraged parents to coview, both formally and by providing content that had some appeal to adults. Finally, they took the time to figure out how preschoolers made sense of the formal features of television; that is, what drew and held their attention. In the end, they created a show in which developmental goals were achieved by using accessible media in a manner consistent with the child's life ecology. This needs to be the lesson learned by earnest educational game designers and researchers.

References

Aldrich, C. (2004). *Simulations and the future of learning*. San Francisco, CA: Pfeiffer.

Bandura, A. (1986). *Social foundations of thought and action*. Englewood Cliffs, NJ: Prentice Hall.

Blumberg, F. C., & Ismailer, S. S. (2009). What do children learn from playing digital games? In U. Ritterfeld, M. Cody, & P. Vorderer (Eds.), *Serious games: Mechanisms and effects* (pp. 131–142). New York, NY: Routledge.

Boot, W. R., Kramer, A. F., Simons, D. J., Fabiani, M., & Gratton, G. (2008). The effects of video game playing on attention, memory, and executive control. *Acta psychologica, 129*(3), 387–398. doi:10.1016/j.actpsy.2008.09.005

Bronfenbrenner, U. (2005). *Making human beings human: Bioecological perspectives on human development*. Thousand Oaks, CA: Sage.

Csikszentmihalyi, M. (1988). The flow experience and its significance for human psychology. In M. Csikszentmihalyi & I. S. Csikszentmihalyi (Eds.), *Optimal experience: Psychological studies of flow in consciousness* (pp. 15–35). New York, NY: Cambridge University Press.

Derry, S. J., & Steinkuehler, C. A. (2003). Cognitive and situative theories of learning and instruction. In L. Nadel (Ed.), *Encyclopedia of cognitive science* (pp. 800–805). England: Nature Publishing Group.

Gee, J. P. (2007). *What video games have to teach us about learning and literacy*. New York, NY: Palmgrave/MacMillan.

Greenberg, B. S., Sherry, J. L., Lachlan, K., Lucas, K., & Holmstrom, A. (2010). Orientations to video games among gender and age groups. *Simulation & Gaming, 41*, 238–259. doi:10.1177/1046878108319930

Hale, S. (1990). A global developmental trend in cognitive processing speed. *Child Development, 61*, 653–663. doi:10.1111/j.1467-8624.1990.tb02809.x

Hartup, W. W., & Stevens, N. (1999). Friendships and adaptation across the life span. *Current Directions in Psychological Science, 8*(3), 76–79. doi:10.1111/1467-8721.00018

Hays, R. T. (2005). *The effectiveness of instructional games: A literature review and discussion*. (No. NAWCTSD-TR-2005-004). Naval Air Warfare Center Training Systems Division, Orlando, FL.

Lerner, R. M. (1978). Nature, nurture, and dynamic interactionism. *Human Development, 21*, 1–20.

Lerner, R. M. (1982). Children and adolescents as producers of their own development. *Developmental Review, 2*, 342–370.

Lisman, J. E., & Grace, A. A. (2005). The hippocampal-VTA loop: Controlling the entry of information into long-term memory. *Neuron, 46*, 703–713.

Mishra, P., & Foster, A. (2007). The claims of games: A comprehensive review and directions for future research. In C. Crawford, D. A. Willis, R. Carlsen, I. Gibson, K. McFerrin, J. Price, & R. Weber (Eds.), *Proceedings of Society for Information Technology & Teacher Education International Conference 2007* (pp. 2227–2232). Chesapeake, VA: AACE.

Mitchell, A., & Savill-Smith, C. (2004). *The use of computer and video games for learning.* London, England: Learning and Skills Development Agency. Retrieved November 1, 2007, from dera.ioe.ac.uk/5270/1/041529.pdf

Olson, C. K. (2010). Children's motivations for video game play in the context of normal development. *Review of General Psychology, 14*(2), 180–187. doi:10.1037/a0018984

Prensky, M. (2000). *Digital game-based learning.* New York, NY: McGraw-Hill.

Ratan, R., & Ritterfeld, U. (2010). Classifying serious games. In U. Ritterfeld, M. Cody, & P. Vorderer (Eds.), *Serious games: Mechanisms and effects* (pp. 10–24). New York, NY: Routledge/LEA.

Ritterfeld, U., Cody, M., & Vorderer, P. (Eds.). (2010). *Serious games: Mechanisms and effects.* New York, NY: Routledge/LEA.

Rosengren, K. E. (1974). Uses and gratifications: A paradigm outlined. In J. G. Blumler & E. Katz (Eds.), *The uses of mass communications: Current perspectives of gratifications research* (pp. 269–286). Beverly Hills, CA: Sage.

Ruggiero, T. E. (2000). Uses and gratifications theory in the 21st century. *Mass Communication and Society, 3*, 3–37. doi:10.1207/S15327825MCS0301_02

Salmon, C. (2000). *Setting a research agenda for entertainment-education.* Atlanta, GA: Centers for Disease Control and Prevention Office of Communication.

Scarr, S., & McCartney, K. (1983). How people make their own environments: A theory of genotype → environment effects. *Child Development, 54*, 424–435. doi:10.2307/1129703

Schmierbach, M., Xu, Q., Oeldorf-Hirsch, A., & Dardis, F. (2012). Electronic friend or virtual foe: Exploring the role of competitive and cooperative multiplayer video game modes in fostering flow and enjoyment. *Media Psychology, 15*, 356–371.

Sherry, J. L. (1997). Prosocial soap operas for development: A review of research and theory. *Journal of International Communication, 4*(2), 75–101.

Sherry, J. L. (2002). Media saturation and entertainment-education. *Communication Theory, 12*, 206–224.

Sherry, J. L. (2004). Flow and media enjoyment. *Communication Theory, 14*(4), 328–347. doi:10.1093/ct/14.4.328

Sherry, J. L., & Dibble, J. (2009). The impact of serious games on childhood development. In U. Ritterfeld, M. Cody, & P. Vorderer (Eds.), *Serious games: Mechanisms and effects* (pp. 145–166). New York, NY: Routledge.

Sherry, J. L., Lucas, K., Greenberg, B., & Lachlan, K. (2006). Video game uses and gratifications as predictors of use and game preference. In P. Vorderer & J. Bryant (Eds.), *Playing computer games: Motives, responses, and consequences* (pp. 248–262). Mahwah, NJ: Erlbaum.

Sherry, J. L., & Pacheco, A. (2006). Matching computer game genres to educational outcomes. *Electronic Journal of Communication.* Retrieved from www.cios.org/EJCPUBLIC/016/1/01615.HTML

Sherry, J. L., Rosaen, S., Bowman, N. D., & Huh, S. (2006, June). *Cognitive skill predicts video game ability.* Paper presented at the annual meeting of the International Communication Association, Dresden, Germany.

Singhal, A., Cody, M. J., Rogers, E. M., & Sabido, M. (Eds.). (2004). *Entertainment-education and social change: History, research, and practice.* Mahwah, NJ: Lawrence Erlbaum Associates.

Singhal, A., & Rogers, E. (1999). *Entertainment-education: A communication strategy for social change*. Mahwah, NJ: Erlbaum.

Spence, I., & Feng, J. (2010). Video games and spatial cognition. *Review of General Psychology, 14*(2), 92–104.

Tomasello, M., Carpenter, M., Call, J., Behne, T., & Moll, H. (2005). Understanding and sharing intentions: The origins of cultural cognition. *Behavioral and Brain Sciences, 28*, 675–691.

Vorderer, P., Hartmann, T., & Klimmt, C. (2003). Explaining the enjoyment of playing video games: The role of competition. In *Proceedings of the Second International Conference on Entertainment Computing* (ICEC '03) (pp. 1–9). Carnegie Mellon University, Pittsburgh, PA.

JOHN L. SHERRY *is an associate in the Department of Communication at Michigan State University, Michigan, USA. He may be reached via e-mail at jsherry@msu.edu.*

Deater-Deckard, K., Chang, M., & Evans, M. E. (2013). Engagement states and learning from educational games. In F. C. Blumberg & S. M. Fisch (Eds.), *Digital Games: A Context for Cognitive Development. New Directions for Child and Adolescent Development, 139,* 21–30.

3

Engagement States and Learning from Educational Games

Kirby Deater-Deckard, Mido Chang, Michael E. Evans

Abstract

Children's and adolescents' cognitive, affective, and behavioral states of engagement enhance or impede enjoyment of, and performance with, educational games. We propose a comprehensive model of engagement states and apply it to research on educational game development and research on the role of various aspects of engagement on game play and learning. Emphasis is placed on individual differences in attention, memory, motor speed and control, persistence, and positive and negative affect (approach/avoidance), and how these pertain to social cognitions regarding mathematics achievement. Our challenge is to develop educational games that are effective for a wide variety of student engagement states. © 2013 Wiley Periodicals, Inc.

Author Note: Funding was provided by the National Science Foundation (DRL-1118571) and the Institute for Society, Culture and Environment (ISCE) at Virginia Tech. Content is solely the responsibility of the authors and does not necessarily represent the official views of the NSF or ISCE. The Learning Transformation Research Group at Virginia Tech includes the authors and our colleagues Osman Balci and Anderson Norton, and a talented team of graduate and undergraduate research assistants.

For youth and adults alike who are using an instructional technology such as an educational game, *engagement* drives moment-by-moment use, as well as the learning that occurs during play and preferably transfers afterwards. Engagement is a collection of mindfully goal-directed states in which motivation arising from positive emotions serves to grab and sustain the learner's cognitive and motor competencies, typically requiring some degree of effort. Engaged learners demonstrate involvement in educational activities through their behavior. These learners also may be more willing to select tasks at the border of their competencies. When given the opportunity they initiate action, persist while they try to do their best, and concentrate on the application of learning new skills and mastering new knowledge. In addition, they often show positive attitudes towards activities including enthusiasm, optimism, curiosity, and interest (Rozendaal, Braat, & Wensveen, 2010).

Engagement is a complex, multifaceted concept. Thus, our aim here is to provide a comprehensive theoretical and practical model of *engagement states* that can guide theory, research, and the development of educational game applications. To this end, we define several subcomponents of engagement and their relevance to student learning during game play, and describe two new measurement tools that flow from this model. Our broader goal is to promote a standardized approach to operationalizing engagement that can inform the development of educational games that maximize appeal and performance across a broad range of students. Outcomes can contribute to the emerging literature on engagement and new media (Small, 2011) and calls for the scientific investigation of multimedia learning (Mayer, 2011).

Engagement and Learning

Engagement is predictive of academic proficiency, motivation, and task persistence, with the balance between learner interest and task demands determining the strength of that engagement (Hoffman & Nadelson, 2010). In theory, if the task is too easy for students, engagement decreases; however, if the task is in a students' range of abilities (in other words, if it is in what Vygotsky called the zone of proximal development; Chaiklin, 2003) and if it is sufficiently challenging, then students' engagement increases. Within this complex system of student motivation and task demands, there is a wide range of individual variation. These individual differences in engagement states are the norm across various stimuli (e.g., visual, auditory) in varying settings (e.g., home, school, at work, and at play) and are predictive of scholastic proficiency and outcomes (Fox, 1994; Posner & Rothbart, 2007).

Engagement states include cognitive, behavioral, and affective components (Skinner & Belmont, 1993). These are summarized in Figure 3.1, which exemplifies our current thinking about "lower-level" engagement

NEW DIRECTIONS FOR CHILD AND ADOLESCENT DEVELOPMENT • DOI: 10.1002/cad

Figure 3.1. Engagement States and Engagement in Mathematics

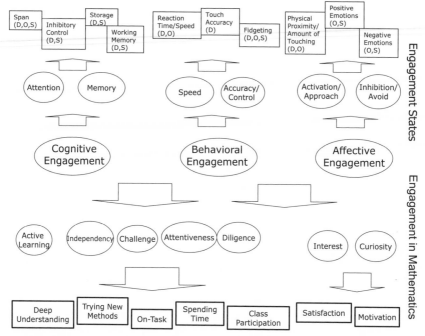

This figure illustrates the various components of cognitive, affective, and behavioral engagement that together produce the wide ranging individual differences seen in the indicators at the top of the figure for engagement states (measured using observations [O], surveys [S], and computer devices [D]), and at the bottom of the figure for higher level engagement in mathematics (measured using surveys).

states (top half of figure, assessed using observation [O], surveys [S], and computer devices [D]) and "higher-level" engagement in mathematics (bottom half of figure, assessed using surveys). Variability in cognitive, behavioral, and affective engagement states arise from variability in nervous and motor system mechanisms that are involved in energy, response to new information (i.e., to approach or withdraw), and regulation of arousal—mechanisms that are part and parcel of successful completion of demanding tasks specifically and learning proficiency generally (Nęcka, 2003). We focus on volitional use of cognitive (attention, memory) and behavioral/motor states that stem from the executive attention and working memory systems and are activated via emotion through behavioral activation and inhibition (Gray, 2000; Kane & Engle, 2003; Posner & Rothbart, 2007).

Cognitive engagement includes attention span/control (i.e., effortful sustained attention), inhibitory control (i.e., effortful withholding of a dominant response to perform a nondominant response), and short-term and working memory. These processes provide voluntary maintenance or suppression of information (Engle, 2002) and are considered as interrelated "executive functions" associated with activation in the frontal lobes (Rueda, Posner, & Rothbart, 2004). Attention and inhibitory control can be measured using interactive game devices and self-reports, as can several closely related aspects of short-term and working memory. For instance, inhibitory control can be assessed using cognitive conflict tasks, whereby the learner must touch a specific object on the screen as a correct response to challenging instructions while also suppressing the impulse to touch other objects that entice attention (i.e., the "pre-potent response"). An example of this is the classic color-word Stroop task, in which one reads color names that are printed in a color that conflicts with the word's meaning (MacLeod, 1991). Initiative/persistence and sustained attentive behavior also can be readily observed during the learner's playing of an educational game. Only children with long attention spans will persist for extended periods of time with a challenging task, as shown in home, school, and laboratory settings (Deater-Deckard & Wang, 2012).

Behavioral (motor) engagement includes speed and accuracy of fine and gross motor movements that involve manipulation of physical or virtual stimuli. These behavioral manifestations of cognitive processing are brought to bear during engagement with stimuli and information, arising from brain stem and motor cortex activations (Posner, 1978). To assess behavioral engagement, motor reaction time arises from brain stem and motor cortex activations and is an excellent direct indicator of the application of cognitive processing speed that is brought to bear during engagement with stimuli and information. Motor reaction time can be measured directly using the game device, based on how quickly the student responds to stimuli on the screen. The speed of correct actions (e.g., cursor moves, screen touches) is a direct measure of reaction time, and the number of incorrect touches also can be recorded and used to interpret reaction time and motor control. Reaction time, speed, and stillness versus fidgeting all can be readily observed as well, just as with sustained attentive behavior described above, to capture the level of each student's behavioral engagement with the game.

Affective engagement captures motivational aspects of approach and avoidance of tools and games, measured as expressions and experiences of positive emotion (e.g., excitement, happiness) and negative emotion (e.g., frustration, irritation, anxiety) states. These affective states have been shown to be critical as enhancements or impediments to effective engagement with, and learning from, educational stimuli (Posner & Rothbart, 2007). Affective engagement is measured from indicators of the learner's approach to or avoidance of the video game. These indicators typically involve vocalizations and facial displays indicative of positive emotions (e.g., excitement, happiness) and negative emotions (e.g., frustration, irritation, anxiety). Observers can readily identify and quantify the degree to which each learner shows positive and negative emotions during game play, as done in a variety of contexts (Deater-Deckard, 2000). Emotions also include an experiential component; thus, it is just as important to assess learners' self-reported positive and negative emotions while playing the game using measures such as the state scale from the Trait-State Anxiety Inventory (Spielberger, 1983). In addition, indirect indicators of affective engagement can be gathered, such as the physical proximity of the learner to the game device.

To develop and test our model of engagement (Figure 3.1), we are studying connections between cognitive, behavioral, and affective engagement states and educational game play in our collaborative research program, The Learning Transformation Research Group @ Virginia Tech. One of the practical features of this program is the development of multiple observational and survey measurement tools for operationalizing individual differences in students' engagement states in classroom settings. This includes the Engagement States Observational Coding System (eSOCS), an instrument designed for systematically observing and quantifying (using 7-point Likert-type scales) various aspects of cognitive, behavioral, and affective engagement. Once validated, we conjecture that it will have broad utility for researchers and practitioners. For example, our engagement model and measurement tool could be used to identify developmental differences in preschool, elementary, middle, and high school learners that would inform modification of new and existing educational games, to make them more developmentally appropriate both for pedagogical and research/assessment activities. We have begun the first large scale study using eSOCS, but we are making it publicly available at our project website, http://ltrg.centers.vt.edu, to receive input from the community to enhance its effectiveness.

Engagement and Scholastic Achievement

Our research team also is focusing on each engagement domain's connection to abstract metacognitive and conscious forms of engagement (e.g., self-concept, self-efficacy) with scholastic subjects; currently we are examining mathematics as an academic domain (Ainley, 1993). Figure 3.1 shows the connection between the three domains of engagement states and the domains of broader engagement in mathematics. In contrast to the lower-level engagement states, higher-level engagement in mathematics captures general tendencies that are temporally more stable and are part of the learner's self-concept, self-efficacy, and sustained motivation to engage and learn mathematics. Engagement in mathematics is categorized into the same three domains as engagement states. Each of these three is thought to range on a continuum of investment or commitment to learning mathematics, from the simple to the complex.

NEW DIRECTIONS FOR CHILD AND ADOLESCENT DEVELOPMENT • DOI: 10.1002/cad

Indicators of cognitive engagement in mathematics include factors of learning, thinking, and problem-solving strategies in mathematics classrooms (Ainley, 1993). The work of Kong, Wong, and Lam (2003) highlights the importance of learning strategies for cognitive engagement in mathematics classes. When learners depend on surface strategies, they memorize formulas rather than show understanding of the underlying principles. When learners resort to deep strategies, students apply mathematics to real life, link the familiar rules to learn new mathematical concepts, understand new concepts thoroughly, and are willing to spend extra hours to deepen understanding in math. In parallel work developing educational games that leverage engagement to improve mathematics proficiency, our approach leads students from application of surface strategy to deep strategy in problem solving and learning challenging concepts that prepare students for challenging mathematics. The promotion and use of learning strategies for deep understanding are well documented in the learning sciences literature (Saxe, 2002).

Behavioral engagement with mathematics can be measured by the degree of the learner's participation in class activities. For example, doing homework, completing class projects (Finn, 1993; Finn & Rock, 1997), following class or school rules (National Center for School Engagement, 2006), and participation in group activities (Newmann, Wehlage, & Lamborn, 1992) serve as examples of engaged behaviors in mathematics. For our efforts, we measure the engaged behaviors as participation in class discussion, concentration when a teacher introduces new concepts, working on problems persistently, and placing extra effort when a problem is not easily solved. Finally, affective engagement in mathematics is assessed based on students' satisfaction, frustration, anxiety, and proficiency orientation. The affective engagement can be measured by the following indicators: student enjoyment of learning mathematics knowledge, feeling curious to learn new things in mathematics, becoming excited when they start a new topic in mathematics, and feeling satisfied when they get good results although learning a new concept may be perceived as tough or boring.

Based on our model of engagement (Figure 3.1), we are developing a survey tool to measure students' mathematics engagement, learner characteristics in educational game settings, educational game engagement, and educational game features. Due to the lack of instruments focusing on mathematics engagement of middle school students, we compiled and compared existing instruments measuring academic engagement on various subjects such as mathematics, social science, and science in K–16 school settings. Using our model of engagement (Figure 3.1), we created survey items that capture three subcomponents of engagement (cognitive, behavioral, and affective) to measure comprehensive mathematical engagement of 5th- and 6th-grade learners in classrooms, to target the age group that is approaching complex prealgebra instruction in middle

NEW DIRECTIONS FOR CHILD AND ADOLESCENT DEVELOPMENT • DOI: 10.1002/cad

school. As an initial validation process to measure the reliability of the instruments, the research team piloted engagement surveys along with mathematical proficiency instruments, work conducted from late 2011 to mid-2012 in a local school district with seven classrooms. The engagement instrument is comprised of 33 items asking students to assess their own engagement levels using four-point Likert scale scores (1 = Really Disagree; 4 = Really Agree).

Like the eSOCS observational tool, the survey tool will be refined and validated through several pilot tests and iterative modification. For the analysis of survey items, advanced measurement models from Classical Test Theory (Traub & Rowley, 1991) and Rasch Theory (Smith & Smith, 2004) have been adopted. Our plan for developing and validating instruments aims for a robust evaluation to measure learners' engagement in consideration of individual differences and educational game features in investigating the potential effects of game play on learning outcomes.

Engagement with Educational Games

Our position is that many children and adolescents are not optimally engaged during academic instruction in mathematics, but this is not the case for video game play. When playing well-designed educational games, most children become deeply involved and engaged. This presents a challenge and an opportunity: Can we connect engagement with educational games and their content to engagement with mathematical concepts and learning in a way that can be rigorously studied and replicated? Moving from the broader definition of engagement described above and in Figure 3.1, a more specific definition of engagement with educational games is "the nexus of intrinsic knowledge and/or interest and external stimuli that promote initial interest in, and continued use of a computer-based learning environment" (Jones, 1998, p. 205). Level of interest is a major aspect of engagement in the game context as it is in the more general sense, because interest represents intrinsic motivation that is primed by external stimuli for learners. The promise of the instructional technology is that educational games can improve students' engagement with their own learning in a way that increases students' proficiency as well as their willingness to attempt frustrating but potentially rewarding experiences in academic subjects that otherwise might not be appealing (Charles, Bustard, & Black, 2009).

As our research team moves forward, the work will focus on two important interrelated questions: 1) Do educational games really have an effect on students' engagement and learning in mathematics? and 2) Does the level of engagement matter for predicting who learns the most from educational games? We are striving to understand how well-designed educational games engage learners, and how these features can be leveraged and used intentionally for positive effects associated with learning academic content (Ritterfeld, Cody, & Vorderer, 2009). One major challenge for all research on engagement with educational games in classroom settings is the generalizability of findings (a challenge that also applies to research on recreational video games). Students who play educational games at school typically report that game play is engaging and motivating, and that they have learned something. Nevertheless, research findings often are not replicated between studies, with some research showing no discernible effects of game play on academic proficiency (Skoric, Teo, & Neo, 2009).

This situation arises in part from the reality that educational games may not be effective for all learners (Van Eck, 2006). Educators need to understand why educational games are engaging and effective. For instance, game features that may engage children and adolescents include high-fidelity graphics and visual effects, memorable music and sound effects, and animations (Jones, 1998). Furthermore, the most engaging game feature typically is the inclusion of a challenging problem to solve, with scaffolds that propel players to a solution. Video games with such features may well provide sufficient challenge and guidance to be engaging, resulting in student-sustained game playing because the games are effective digitally enhanced learning environments (Malone, 1981). We know that developers of entertainment video games often get it right. As researchers in psychology and education, we strive to understand how these features can be appropriated for intentional learning experiences (Gee, 2008; Honey & Hilton, 2011).

Yet even with ideally designed and delivered educational games, individual differences in engagement will remain. For those of us who study individual differences in learning, this juxtaposition places us at an exciting point in the evolution of a research agenda, as shown in the current collection of papers. To move forward effectively, we will need investigations of the variability in student engagement and motivation with educational games (Kebritchi, Hirumi & Bai, 2010). It is this line of inquiry, with a focus on identifying the causes and consequences of individual differences in engagement with educational games, that could revolutionize the way in which video game technology enhances learning and educational attainment outcomes for students from many background and ability levels.

References

Ainley, M. D. (1993). Styles of engagement with learning: Multidimensional assessment of their relationship with strategy use and school achievement. *Journal of Educational Psychology, 85*(3), 395–405.

Chaiklin, S. (2003). The zone of proximal development in Vygotsky's analysis of learning and instruction. In A. Kozulin, B. Gindis, V. Ageyev, & S. Miller (Eds.), *Vygotsky's educational theory and practice in cultural context* (pp. 39–64). Cambridge, England: Cambridge University Press.

Charles, M., Bustard, D., & Black, M. (2009). Experiences of promoting engagement in game-based learning. In *Proceedings of the European Conference on Games Based Learning* (pp. 397–403). Retrieved from Education Research Complete database.

Deater-Deckard, K. (2000). Parenting and child behavioral adjustment in early childhood: A quantitative genetic approach to studying family processes and child development. *Child Development, 71*, 468–484.

Deater-Deckard, K., & Wang, Z. (2012). Development of temperament and attention: Behavioral genetic approaches. In M. Posner (Ed.), *Cognitive neuroscience of attention* (2nd ed.). New York, NY: Guilford.

Engle, R. W. (2002). Working memory capacity as executive attention. *Current Directions in Psychological Science, 11*, 19–23.

Finn, J. D. (1993). *School engagement and students at risk.* Washington, DC: National Center for Education Statistics.

Finn, J. D., & Rock, D. A. (1997). Academic success among students at risk for school failure. *Journal of Applied Psychology, 82*, 221–234.

Fox, N. A. (Ed.). (1994). Dynamic cerebral processes underlying emotion regulation. In *The development of emotion regulation: Biological and behavioral considerations* (pp. 152–166). *Monographs of the Society for Research in Child Development, 59* (2–3, Serial No. 240).

Gee, J. P. (2008). Learning and games. In K. Salen (Ed.), *The Ecology of games: Connecting youth, games, and learning* (pp. 21–40). Cambridge, MA: The MIT Press.

Gray, W. D. (2000). The nature and processing of errors in interactive behavior. *Cognitive Science, 24*(2), 205–248.

Hoffman, B., & Nadelson, L. (2010). Motivational engagement and video gaming: A mixed methods study. *Educational Technology Research & Development, 58*, 245–270. doi:10.1007/s11423-009-9134-9

Honey, M. A., & Hilton, M. L. (2011). *Learning science through computer games and simulations.* Washington, DC: National Academies Press.

Jones, M. G. (1998, February). Creating electronic learning environments: Games, flow and the user interface. In *Proceedings of selected research and development presentations at the national convention of the association for educational communications and technology (AECT)*, St. Louis, MO.

Kane, M. J., & Engle, R. W. (2003). Working memory capacity and the control of attention: The contributions of goal neglect, response competition, and task set to Stroop interference. *Journal of Experimental Psychology: General, 132*, 47–70.

Kebritchi, M., Hirumi, A., & Bai, H. (2010). The effects of modern mathematics computer games on mathematics achievement and class motivation. *Computers & Education, 55*, 427–443.

Kong, Q., Wong, N., & Lam, C. (2003). Student engagement in mathematics: Development of instrument and validation of construct. *Mathematics Education Research Journal, 15*, 4–21.

MacLeod, C. M. (1991). Half a century of research on the Stroop effect: An integrative review. *Psychological Bulletin, 109*, 163–203.

Malone, T. W. (1981). Toward a theory of intrinsically motivating instruction. *Cognitive Science, 5*, 333–369.

Mayer, R. E. (2011). Toward a science of motivated learning in technology-supported environments. *Educational Technology Research & Development, 59*(2), 301–308.

National Center for School Engagement. (2006). *Quantifying school engagement: Research Report.* Denver, CO: Colorado Foundation for Families and Children.

Nęcka, E. (2003). Creative interaction: A conceptual schema for the process of producing ideas and judging the outcomes. In M. A. Runco (Ed.), *Critical Creative Processes* (pp. 115–127). Hampton Press.

Newmann, F. M., Wehlage, G. G., & Lamborn, S. D. (1992). The significance and sources of student engagement. In F. M. Newmann (Ed.), *Student engagement and achievement in American secondary schools* (pp. 11–39). New York, NY: Teachers College Press.

Posner, M. I. (1978). *Chronometric explorations of mind.* Hillsdale, NJ: Erlbaum.

Posner, M. I., & Rothbart, M. K. (2007). *Educating the human brain.* Washington, DC: American Psychological Association.

Ritterfeld, U., Cody, M., & Vorderer, P. (2009). *Serious games: Mechanisms and effects.* New York, NY: Routledge.

Rozendaal, M., Braat, B., & Wensveen, S. (2010). Exploring sociality and engagement in play through game-control distribution. *AI & Society, 25,* 193–201. doi:10.1007/s00146-009-0245-y

Rueda, M. R., Posner, M. I., & Rothbart, M. K. (2004). Attentional control and self-regulation. In R. F. Baumeister & K. D. Vohs (Eds.), *Handbook of self-regulation: Research, theory, and applications* (pp. 283–300). New York, NY: Guilford.

Saxe, G. (2002). Children's developing mathematics in collective practices: A framework for analysis. *The Journal of Learning Sciences, 11,* 275–300.

Skinner, E., & Belmont, M. (1993). Motivation in the classroom: Reciprocal effects of teacher behavior and student engagement across the school year. *Journal of Educational Psychology, 85,* 571–581. doi:10.1037/0022-0663.85.4.571

Skoric, M., Teo, L., & Neo, R. (2009). Children and video games: Addiction, engagement, and scholastic achievement. *CyberPsychology & Behavior, 12*(5), 567–572. doi:10.1089/cpb.2009.0079

Small, R. (2011). Motivation and new media: An introduction to the special issue. *Educational Technology Research & Development, 59,* 177–180.

Smith, E. V., Jr., & Smith, R. M. (2004). *Introduction to Rasch measurement: Theory, models, and applications.* Maple Grove, MN: JAM Press.

Spielberger, C. D. (1983). *Manual for the State-Trait Anxiety Inventory (STAI).* Palo Alto, CA: Consulting Psychologists Press.

Traub, R. E., & Rowley, G. L. (1991). Understanding reliability. *Educational Measurement: Issues and Practice, 10,* 37–45. doi:10.1111/j.1745-3992.1991.tb00183.x

Van Eck, R. (2006). Digital game-based learning: It's not just the digital natives who are restless. *EDUCAUSE Review, 41,* 16–30.

KIRBY DEATER-DECKARD *is professor of psychology and psychiatry at Virginia Tech, Blacksburg, Virginia, USA, and can be reached via e-mail at kirbydd@vt.edu.*

MIDO CHANG *is associate professor of leadership and professional studies at Florida International University, Miami, Florida, USA, and can be reached via e-mail at midchang@fiu.edu.*

MICHAEL E. EVANS *is associate professor of learning sciences and technologies at Virginia Tech, Blacksburg, Virginia, USA, and can be reached via e-mail at mae@vt.edu.*

Revelle, G. (2013). Applying developmental theory and research to the creation of educational games. In F. C. Blumberg & S. M. Fisch (Eds.), *Digital Games: A Context for Cognitive Development. New Directions for Child and Adolescent Development, 139*, 31–40.

4

Applying Developmental Theory and Research to the Creation of Educational Games

Glenda Revelle

Abstract

The field of developmental psychology has produced abundant theory and research about the physical, cognitive, social, and emotional development of children; however, to date there has been limited use of this wealth of knowledge by developers creating games for children. This chapter provides an overview of key theoretical observations and research-based insight regarding children's development and outlines practical implications for their application to game design. © 2013 Wiley Periodicals, Inc.

Introduction

The advent of personal computers in the early 1980s brought about the development of computer software designed specifically for children. The first widely known effort to apply developmental theory and principles to software for children was that of Seymour Papert. Early in his career, Papert worked with Piaget, and later applied Piaget's constructivist theory of development (e.g., Piaget, 1952) to the domain of learning/interacting with computers, dubbing this approach "constructionism" (Papert, 1980). Piaget theorized that children actively "construct" their own knowledge in interaction with the world around them, progressively internalizing their actions and the results of those actions. Papert applied that theory to digital learning environments and extended it, arguing that learning (construction of knowledge) is optimized when the learner is literally constructing or making something in the digital world.

Papert and colleagues' development of the Logo programming language (Feurzeig & Papert, 1968) exemplified this approach, enabling children to create computer programs. Well-known constructionist projects that emerged from the thinking of Papert, his colleagues, and his students include LEGO®Mindstorms (Resnick, Martin, Sargent, & Silverman, 1996), Alan Kay's Squeak (Ingalls, Kaehler, Maloney, Wallace, & Kay, 1997), Mitch Resnick's Scratch (Resnick et al., 2009), computationally-enhanced construction kits (Eisenberg, Eisenberg, Gross, Kaowthumrong, Lee, & Lovett, 2002), and the "Children as Design Partners" model of research and development (Druin, 2002).

Child Development and Interface Design

There has long been an interest in applying developmental knowledge to interface design (Grover, 1986; Haugland & Shade, 1990). A computer game's "interface"—the system of hardware (e.g., mouse, joystick, touchscreen) and software functions (e.g., point-and-click, drag, scroll) used to access and interact with the game—can serve to either facilitate or hinder game play. For children, whose motor and cognitive abilities are still developing, difficulty using the interface can often impede engagement with the game.

Strommen (1993) proposed a cognitive model of device difficulty, in which he suggested that there are two additive components of cognitive load with regard to input device use: the degree to which movement of the device for cursor control parallels the movements used in human pointing, and the number of "rules-of-use" of the device. His analysis predicted that on initial use, the trackball should be easier to use than the mouse, which in turn should be easier than the joystick, an ordering that is consistent with results of early empirical studies with children (Jones, 1991; King & Alloway, 1992; Revelle & Strommen, 1990). Strommen's model predicted that the easiest device for young children to use should be a touchscreen, foreshadowing by almost two decades the tremendous popularity and success of tablet and mobile touchscreen interfaces for young children.

The Mouse. Ever since the mouse-driven point-and-click interface became standard for computer systems, most of the research has focused on factors influencing young children's ability to use the mouse (see reviews by Lane & Ziviani, 1997, 2010). Hourcade, Bederson, Druin and Guimbretiere (2004) integrated relevant research and theory in the areas of child development (Kail, 1991) and human–computer interaction (Card, Moran, & Newell, 1983) to explain the impact of children's developing cognitive and motor skills on their ability to use the mouse. Because children's reaction times are slower, meaning their information processing times are longer, the theoretically-based prediction is that children's cursor path trajectories to the target would be less direct, less accurate, and take longer than those of adults. Confirming these predictions, Hourcade and colleagues (2004) found that age had significant effects on accuracy, efficiency, and frequency of target re-entry (the result of overshooting the target and then coming back) for 4- and 5-year-olds; Lambert and Bard (2005) found similar age effects for 6- to 10-year-olds. Both of these studies, along with Donker and Reitsma (2007), found that increasing target size (compared with the target size needed for adults) can improve children's efficiency and accuracy.

Alternative Input Devices. There are strong developmental reasons why certain alternative hardware interfaces are both easier for children to use and more developmentally appropriate than the mouse. This section highlights three interfaces that have particularly child-appropriate attributes.

Tangible Interfaces. It has long been theorized that young children's play with physical objects is crucial to cognitive development (cf., Piaget, 1952; Vygotsky, 1978). These objects can include general purpose objects, such as sticks or rocks that the child uses imaginatively, or objects especially designed to be toys, like dolls, toy cars, or toy food items.

Tangible interfaces provide digital interactivity and contingent feedback through real physical objects that are relevant to the task or game, instead of a mouse with a computer screen. Researchers have developed a variety of tangible interfaces for children's interactive experiences (see review by Zaman, Abeele, Markopoulos, & Marshall, 2012). Embedding interactivity into physical objects enables children's play with physical toys to be supported, extended, and enhanced by the contingent feedback and other learning supports that can be provided by digital technology.

In one direct comparison of children's use of a mouse-based interface versus a tangible interface for solving a jigsaw puzzle task, Antle, Droumeva, and Ha (2009) found that 7- to 10-year-old children were more successful, faster, and more strategic in their problem solving when using the tangible interface than with the mouse-based input. However, as Zaman and colleagues (2012) noted, much of the work on tangible interfaces and children has been theoretically driven or design-driven. There have been few empirical validation studies, and among extant evaluative studies there are equivocal findings regarding the superiority of tangible interfaces. As Zaman and colleagues suggest, the advantages or disadvantages of tangible input are likely dependent on the context and goals of the interactive experience.

Touchscreens. Strommen's previously mentioned cognitive model of device difficulty (1993) hypothesized that the touchscreen should be the easiest interface for young children to use. Since the iPhone and iPad and other tablet devices have been released, ample anecdotal evidence would seem to support this prediction. For young children, the recent widespread availability of touchscreen interfaces is of major significance.

For the first time in the history of digital interactivity, there is a commonly available interface that very young children can use effectively. Until now, for the youngest children it didn't really matter that the American Academy of Pediatrics' (2001, 2011) directives (no "screen time" for children under age two and a limit of 1–2 hours per day for older children) made no distinction between time spent watching linear video versus time spent engaged in interactivity, since they typically weren't able to use the interfaces that were available. Now that touchscreens are commonly available and seem to be easy for young children to use, there is a call-to-action for research on the effects (positive and/or negative) of using various kinds of screen-based interactive applications on young children's development.

Whole Body Movement. The Wii, Kinect, and other interfaces that detect users' body movements provide another opportunity for more intuitive interaction styles. Engaging children in whole body learning experiences while playing games is consistent with the theoretical construct of embodied cognition: the idea that thinking and learning is heavily influenced by the physical form and movement of the human body. Embodied cognition theory (e.g., Wilson, 2002) assumes that the human mind has evolved to learn in physical interaction with the environment, a complementary notion to Piaget's (1952) idea that a central component of cognitive development is infants' and toddlers' coordination of their sensory inputs with motor responses.

From a theoretical perspective, embodied interaction (in which physical body movements are used to interact with technology) has the potential to support learning. Researchers have recently built embodied-interaction systems designed to help young students learn about proportions (Howison, Trninic, Reinholz, & Abrahamson, 2011), numerical magnitude (Cress, Fischer, Moeller, Sauter, & Nuerk, 2010), and musical concepts (Antle, Corness, & Droumeva, 2009). The use of full-body physical movement in game play has also been linked to increased engagement

(Bianchi-Berthouze, Kim, & Patel, 2007; Ibister & DiMauro, 2011) and social interaction (Lindley, Couteur, & Bianchi-Berthouze, 2008).

Whole-body movement interfaces could also contribute to motor development. During early childhood, gross motor skills develop rapidly. Between the ages of 3 and 5, children typically progress from engaging in simple gross motor events like running or standing on one foot to more complex activities requiring much greater balance and coordination, like riding a scooter or skating. During this time, children are described as having a "high motor drive," meaning that they enjoy engaging in gross motor activity like jumping, spinning, and running around for the sheer pleasure of it. To the extent that this high motor drive can be engaged in a learning game, both motor and cognitive development can be enhanced.

There has also been much speculation about the promise of whole-body movement interfaces to get older children "up off the couch" and engage them in higher levels of physical activity to help combat the childhood obesity epidemic (see Calvert, Staiano, & Bond, this volume). Unfortunately, results of at least one recent study indicate that simply introducing games that require physical activity into families' homes without any prescription for their use does not lead to increased levels of physical activity in children ages 9–12 (Baranowski et al., 2012). Further research is needed examining factors that might lead to better outcomes in this regard, including investigating how game design might influence children's interest and motivation to engage over time in games that require physical activity.

Child Development and Game Features

Recent efforts have been made to convey child development information to game designers and developers. Bekker and Antle (2011) created a set of "developmentally-situated design cards" to aid developers in understanding the cognitive, social, emotional, and physical development of children in various age groups. Each card also provides examples of activities that address the skill in age-appropriate fashion. Carla Fisher (e.g., 2012) has made a number of presentations to convey child development principles to game designers. This kind of knowledge has positive implications for the developmental appropriateness of game design and the likelihood that children in the target age range will enjoy and learn from the game.

Leveling and Hints/Clues. One particularly effective approach to supporting children's learning is via scaffolding, the provision of learning support by a mentor (e.g., Vygotsky, 1978). Scaffolding has been shown to be an effective learning tool when used by teachers (Berk & Winsler, 1995; Bodrova & Leong, 2006). Further, many parents naturally use scaffolding when interacting with their children (Pratt, Green, MacVicar, & Bountrogianni, 1992; Pratt, Kerig, Cowan, & Cowan, 1988), and recent research (Hammond, Muller, Carpendale, Bibok, & Liebermann-Finestone,

2012) indicates that parents' use of scaffolding can enhance children's executive function and verbal ability.

In the context of digital games, scaffolding is a particularly useful technique for supporting children of varying ability levels in playing the same game and has frequently been used effectively in educational software (Pea, 2004; Revelle, 2003). Scaffolding has been incorporated into games in two primary ways: leveling and hints or clues. Computer games almost always include a sequence of game levels that increase in difficulty as the player becomes more proficient and advances in the game. Learning is enhanced by increasing the cognitive demands as game levels progress, rather than simply the demand on psychomotor skills (manual dexterity or eye-hand coordination). Accordingly, early levels provide more scaffolding for children's learning, which is gradually removed as the player progresses through game levels.

The child's selection of a wrong answer also provides an opportunity for scaffolding support. When the child makes an incorrect choice, the game can provide additional support in the form of hints or clues for approaching the problem. These clues can offer progressively more help with each subsequent mistake, until the child is capable of solving the problem. Revelle, Medoff, & Strommen (2001) provide a thorough description of the process for incorporating scaffolding for learning within children's educational games.

Motivation. Ever since there have been computer games, researchers have been asking what makes them "fun," or instrinsically motivating (e.g., Malone & Lepper, 1987); that is, why do children want to play them on their own with no encouragement, prompting, or external motivation? Much earlier, Deci (1971) argued that some activities provide their own "inherent" reward, independent of extrinsic rewards to sustain or increase their occurrence. Well-designed computer games exemplify this type of activity.

What are the properties of computer games that prompt children to be intrinsically motivated to play? von Salisch, Oppl, and Kristen (2006) suggest that children are motivated to select games that address developmental issues that they are facing at the time. An ethnographic study of video game play in the context of children's real, everyday lives by Stevens, Satwicz, and McCarthy (2008) concluded that the role of game play is too complex and varied to expect that there would be isolable properties that account for a single motivation to play. Olson (2010) takes it a step further, examining the multiple motivations for game play and the various ways in which developmental stage and level of cognitive development may influence which games are particularly appealing and motivating for different children, confirming that playing video games serves a diverse array of needs throughout childhood and adolescence.

Theorists and researchers have compared students with extrinsically motivated "performance orientations," based on external incentives such as school grades or parental rewards, to those with intrinsically motivated "mastery orientations," based on the internal drive to do one's best or to meet one's own goals. Research (e.g., Anderman, Austin, & Johnson, 2002) shows that long-term school success is greatest for those driven by intrinsic motivation. Many of the studies reviewed by Jennings & Dietz (2003) indicate that mastery motivation also enhances cognitive development. Accordingly, there have been efforts to understand what is intrinsically motivating about games, and how to bring those dynamics into the classroom (e.g., Dickey, 2005; Gee, 2007).

How children perceive the concept of "intelligence" also impacts their response to challenge, persistence, and performance. According to Dweck and colleagues (e.g., Dweck & Master, 2009) some children view intelligence as a fixed quantity of "smartness" that is relatively intractable, whereas others have an incremental or growth view of intelligence that is malleable via effort. Dweck's research has shown that children with a growth mind-set are more likely to take risks, try new approaches, and persist at challenging tasks, all of which lead to improved performance over the more conservative approaches of those with a fixed mind-set. Moreover, the wording of praise for children's accomplishments may affect which mind-set is promoted in development. Praise for one's effort and progress is more likely to encourage a growth mind-set, whereas praise for one's task performance or ability is more likely to encourage a fixed mind-set. This finding has important implications for the wording of reward messages in children's games.

Conclusion

Under the approach known as *user-centered design*, the design of interactive technology takes as its starting point not the capabilities of the technology but, rather, the needs of its prospective users. In the case of interactive games for children, informing design with an understanding of the developmental needs, abilities, and challenges of children in various age groups can significantly improve the games' usability, appeal, and effectiveness, maximizing engagement and learning.

References

American Academy of Pediatrics. (2001). Children, adolescents, and television. *Pediatrics, 107*(2), 423–426.

American Academy of Pediatrics. (2011). Policy statement: Media use by children younger than two years. *Pediatrics, 128*(5), 1040–1045.

Anderman, E., Austin, C., & Johnson, D. (2002). The development of goal orientation. In A. Wigfield and J. Eccles (Eds.), *Development of achievement motivation* (pp. 197–220). San Diego, CA: Academic Press.

Antle, A., Corness, G., & Droumeva, M. (2009). What the body knows: Exploring the benefits of embodied metaphors in hybrid physical digital environments. *Interacting with Computers, 21*(1–2), 66–75.

Antle, A. N., Droumeva, M., & Ha, D. (2009). Hands on what? Comparing children's mouse-based and tangible-based interaction. In *Proceedings of the 8th International Conference on Interaction Design and Children 2009* (pp. 80–88). New York, NY: ACM.

Baranowski, T., Abdelsamad, D., Baranowski, J., O'Connor, T., Thompson, D., Barnett, A., . . . Chen, T. (2012). Impact of an active video game on healthy children's physical activity. *Pediatrics, 129*(3), 636–642.

Bekker, T., & Antle, A. (2011). Developmentally situated design (DSD): Making theoretical knowledge accessible to designers of children's technology. In *Proceedings of the 2011 Annual Conference on Human Factors in Computing Systems* (pp. 2531–2540). New York, NY: ACM.

Berk, L. E., & Winsler, A. (1995). *Scaffolding children's learning: Vygotsky and early childhood education.* Washington, DC: NAEYC.

Bianchi-Berthouze, N., Kim, W., & Patel, D. (2007). Does body movement engage you more in digital game play, and why? In A. Paiva, R. Prada, & R. Picard (Eds.), *Affective Computing and Intelligent Interaction* (pp. 102–113). Berlin/Heidelberg, Germany: Springer.

Bodrova, E., & Leong, D. (Eds.). (2006). *Tools of the mind: The Vygotskyian approach to early childhood education.* New York, NY: Prentice Hall.

Card, S., Moran, T., & Newell, A. (1983). *The psychology of human–computer interaction.* Hillsdale, NJ: Lawrence Erlbaum Associates.

Cress, U., Fischer, U., Moeller, K., Sauter, C., & Nuerk, H. (2010). The use of a digital dance mat for training kindergarten children in a magnitude comparison task. *Proceedings of the 9th International Conference of the Learning Sciences, Vol. 1,* 105–112.

Deci, E. L. (1971). Effects of externally mediated rewards on intrinsic motivation. *Journal of Personality and Social Psychology, 18,* 105–115.

Dickey, M. (2005). Engaging by design: How engagement strategies in popular computer and video games can inform instructional design. *Educational Technology Research and Development, 53*(2), 67–83.

Donker, A., & Reitsma, P. (2007). Aiming and clicking in young children's use of the computer mouse. *Computers in Human Behavior, 23,* 2863–2874.

Druin, A. (2002). The role of children in the design of new technology. *Behaviour and Information Technology, 21*(1), 1–25.

Dweck, C. S., & Master, A. (2009). Self-theories and motivation: Student beliefs about intelligence. In K. Wenzel & A. Wigfield (Eds.), *Handbook of motivation at school* (pp. 123–140). New York, NY: Routledge.

Eisenberg, M., Eisenberg, A., Gross, M., Kaowthumrong, K., Lee, N., & Lovett, W. (2002). Computationally enhanced construction kits for children: Prototype and principles. In *Proceedings of ICLS (International Conference on the Learning Sciences),* 79–85.

Feurzeig, W., & Papert, S. (1968). Programming languages as a conceptual framework for teaching mathematics. *Proceedings of NATO Science Conference on Computers and Learning,* 37–42.

Fisher, C. (2012, March). *Little hands, foul moods, and runny noses: Developmental research meets emerging technologies.* Presentation at Game Developers Conference (GDC 12), San Francisco, CA.

Gee, J. P. (2007). *What videogames have to teach us about learning and literacy* (Rev. ed.). New York, NY: Palgrave Macmillan.

Grover, S. (1986). A field study of the use of cognitive-developmental principles in microcomputer design for young children. *Journal of Educational Research, 79*(6), 325–331.

Hammond, S., Muller, U., Carpendale, J., Bibok, M., & Liebermann-Finestone, D. (2012). The effects of parental scaffolding on preschoolers' executive function. *Developmental Psychology, 48*(1), 271–281.

Haugland, S., & Shade, D. (1990). *Developmental evaluations of software for young children*. Albany, NY: Delmar Publishers, Inc.

Hourcade, J., Bederson, B., Druin, A., & Guimbretiere, F. (2004). Differences in pointing task performance between preschool children and adults using mice. *ACM Transactions on Computer Human Interaction, 11*(4), 357–386.

Howison, M., Trninic, D., Reinholz, D., & Abrahamson, D. (2011). The mathematical imagery trainer: From embodied interaction to conceptual learning. In *Proceedings of the 2011 annual conference on human factors in computing systems* (pp. 1989–1998). New York, NY: ACM.

Isbister, K., & DiMauro, C. (2011). Waggling the form baton: Analyzing body-movement-based design patterns in Nintendo Wii games. In D. England (Ed.), *Whole Body Interaction* (pp. 63–73). London, England: Springer.

Ingalls, D., Kaehler, T., Maloney, J., Wallace, S., & Kay, A. (1997). Back to the future: The story of Squeak, a practical Smalltalk written in itself. In *Proceedings of the 12th ACM SIGPLAN Conference on Object-Oriented Programming, Systems, Languages, and Applications* (pp. 318–326). New York: ACM.

Jennings, K., & Dietz, L. (2003). Mastery motivation and goal persistence in young children. In M. Bornstein, L. Davidson, C. Keyes, & K. Moore (Eds.), *Well-being: Positive development across the life course* (pp. 295–309). Mahwah, NJ: Lawrence Erlbaum and Associates.

Jones, T. (1991). An empirical study of children's use of computer pointing devices. *Journal of Educational Computing Research, 7*(1), 61–76.

Kail, R. (1991). Developmental change in speed of processing during childhood and adolescence. *Psychological Bulletin, 109*(3), 490–501.

King, J., & Alloway, N. (1992). Preschoolers' use of microcomputers and input devices. *Journal of Educational Computing Research, 8*(4), 451–468.

Lambert, J., & Bard, C. (2005). Acquisition of visuomanual skills and improvement of information processing capacities in 6- to 10-year-old children performing a 2D pointing task. *Neuroscience Letters, 377*, 106.

Lane, A., & Ziviani, J. (1997). The suitability of the mouse for children's use: A review of the literature. *Journal of Computing in Childhood Education, 8*(2/3), 227–245.

Lane, A., & Ziviani, J. (2010). Factors influencing skilled use of a computer mouse by school-aged children. *Computers & Education, 55*(3), 1112–1122.

Lindley, S., Couteur, J., & Bianchi-Berthouze, N. (2008). Stirring up experience through movement in game play: Effects on engagement and social behaviour. In *Proceedings of the 26th Annual SIGCHI Conference on Human Factors in Computing Systems* (pp. 511–514). Florence, Italy.

Malone, T., & Lepper, M. (1987). Making learning fun: A taxonomy of intrinsic motivations for learning. In R. Snow & M. Farr (Eds.), *Aptitude, learning, and instruction: Vol. 3. Conative and affective process analyses* (pp. 223–253). Hillsdale, NJ: Lawrence Erlbaum.

Olson, C. (2010). Children's motivations for video game play in the context of normal development. *Review of General Psychology, 14*(2), 180–187.

Papert, S. (1980). *Mindstorms: Children, computers, and powerful ideas*. New York, NY: Basic Books.

Pea, R. D. (2004). The social and technological dimensions of scaffolding and related theoretical concepts for learning, education, and human activity. *Journal of Learning Sciences, 13*(3), 423–451.

Piaget, J. (1952). *Origins of intelligence in children*. New York, NY: International Universities Press.

Pratt, M., Green, D., MacVicar, J., & Bountrogianni, M. (1992). The mathematical parent: Parental scaffolding, parenting style, and learning outcomes in long-division mathematics homework. *Journal of Applied Developmental Psychology, 13*(1), 17–34.

Pratt, M., Kerig, P., Cowan, P., & Cowan, C. (1988). Mothers and fathers teaching 3-year-olds: Authoritative parenting and adult scaffolding of young children's learning. *Developmental Psychology*, *24*(6), 832–839.

Resnick, M., Maloney, J., Monroy-Hernandez, A., Rusk, N., Eastmond, E., Brennan, K., . . . Kafai, Y. (2009). Scratch: Programming for all. *Communications of the ACM*, *52*(11), 60–67.

Resnick, M., Martin, F., Sargent, R., & Silverman, B. (1996). Programmable bricks: Toys to think with. *IBM Systems Journal*, *35*(3–4), 443–452.

Revelle, G. (2003). Educating via entertainment media: The Sesame Workshop approach. *Computers in Entertainment*, *1*(1). doi:10.1145/950566.950590

Revelle, G., Medoff, L., & Strommen, E. (2001). Interactive technologies research at Children's Television Workshop. In S. Fisch & R. Truglio (Eds.), *"G" is for growing: Thirty years of research on* Sesame Street (pp. 215–230). Mahwah, NJ: Lawrence Erlbaum Associates.

Revelle, G., & Strommen, E. (1990). The effects of practice and input device used on young children's computer control. *Journal of Computing in Childhood Education*, *2*(1), 33–41.

Stevens, R., Satwicz, T., & McCarthy, L. (2008). In-game, in-room, in-world: Reconnecting video game play to the rest of kids' lives. In K. Salen (Ed.), *The Ecology of Games: Connecting Youth, Games, and Learning* (pp. 41–66). Cambridge, MA: The MIT Press.

Strommen, E. (1993). Preschool children at the interface: A cognitive model of device difficulty. *Proceedings of the 15th Annual Convention of the Association for Educational Communications and Technology*, 991–999.

von Salisch, M., Oppl, C., & Kristen, A. (2006). What attracts children? In P. Vorderer & J. Bryant (Eds.), *Playing video games: Motives, responses and consequences* (pp. 147–163). Hillsdale, NJ: Erlbaum.

Vygotsky, L. (1978). *Mind in society: The development of higher psychological processes*. Cambridge, MA: Harvard University Press.

Wilson, M. (2002). Six views of embodied cognition. *Psychonomic Bulletin & Review*, *9*(4), 625–636.

Zaman, B., Abeele, V., Markopoulos, P., & Marshall, P. (2012). Editorial: The evolving field of tangible interaction for children: The challenge of empirical validation. From Tangible Interaction and Children [Special Issue], *Personal and Ubiquitous Computing*, *16*(4), 367–378.

GLENDA REVELLE is associate professor of human development and family sciences in the School of Human Environmental Sciences, Dale Bumpers College of Agricultural, Food and Life Sciences at the University of Arkansas, Arkansas, USA, and can be reached via e-mail at grevelle@uark.edu.

Blumberg, F. C., Altschuler, E. A., Almonte, D. E., & Mileaf, M. I. (2013). The impact of recreational video game play on children's and adolescents' cognition. In F. C. Blumberg & S. M. Fisch (Eds.), *Digital Games: A Context for Cognitive Development. New Directions for Child and Adolescent Development, 139*, 41–50.

5

The Impact of Recreational Video Game Play on Children's and Adolescents' Cognition

Fran C. Blumberg, Elizabeth A. Altschuler, Debby E. Almonte, Maxwell I. Mileaf

Abstract

Current empirical findings show linkages between recreational video game play and enhanced cognitive skills, primarily among young adults. However, consideration of this linkage among children and adolescents is sparse. Thus, discussions about facilitating transfer of cognitive skills from video game play to academic tasks among children and adolescents remains largely uninformed by research. To inform this discussion, we review available research concerning the cognitive benefits of video game play among children and adolescents and their impressions of video games as learning tools as these impressions may impact their application of cognitive skills used during game play to academic tasks. © 2013 Wiley Periodicals, Inc.

New Directions for Child and Adolescent Development, no. 139, Spring 2013 © Wiley Periodicals, Inc.
Published online in Wiley Online Library (wileyonlinelibrary.com). • DOI: 10.1002/cad.20030

A growing literature has documented the benefits, rather than the perils, of video game play (see Blumberg, 2011; Ferguson, 2010; Salonius-Pasternak & Gelfond, 2005). One impetus for this emphasis is the continuing popularity of digital game play among players of all ages and both genders. For example, 2012 industry data from the Entertainment Software Association indicated that 49% of U.S. households owned at least one dedicated game console and that 47% of all game players were female, as compared with 42% in 2011 (Entertainment Software Association, 2012). Another impetus is the keen interest of educators (see Gee, 2003; Squire, 2008) and funding agencies (e.g., MacArthur Foundation Digital Media Digital Learning Initiative, 2012) in capitalizing on the strong appeal of video game play for educational use in formal and informal learning settings. This interest is fueled by findings attesting to the linkage between frequent recreational video game play and enhancements in inductive reasoning (Greenfield, Camaioni, Ercolani, Weiss, Lauber, & Perucchini, 1994; Pillay, 2002), mental rotation and spatial visualization (Okagaki & Frensch, 1994), spatial distribution of attention and visual selective attention (Boot, Kramer, Simons, Fabiani, & Gratton, 2008; Green & Bavelier, 2003, 2006a, 2006b, 2007; Karle, Watter, & Shedden, 2010), and memory (Boot et al., 2008). More recently, the playing of exergames, a relatively new genre of video games that incorporate exercise as part of game play, has been shown to promote executive functioning as reflected by skills such as task switching and perceptual speed (Staiano, Abraham, & Calvert, 2012; also see Calvert, Staiano, & Bond, this volume).

These linkages are largely documented in studies conducted with young adults, rather than children and adolescents. However, nearly one third of all players (32%) are younger than age 18 (Entertainment Software Association, 2012) and 97% of 12- to 17-year-olds are reported to play video games (Lehrman, 2012). Further, recent findings show that 8- to 14-year-olds are playing, on average, more than an hour per day (see Rideout, Foehr, & Roberts, 2010).

Our goal here is to briefly review what is known about the cognitive impact of recreational video game play among children and adolescents. This body of research is fairly sparse and largely based in the education and educational technology literature (see Blumberg, 2011). The paucity of research in developmental psychology journals is surprising, as video game play continues to grow as a context in which children and adolescents spend their time and interact with one another. One could argue that children's and adolescents' expanding media use overall (see Rideout et al., 2010) and video game play in particular provides a context in which cognitive development is promoted (see Greenfield, 1994) and thereby is worthy of developmental psychologists' examination.

Apart from its relevance to the study of cognitive development, this review also holds value for informing the design of *serious games*. These games are characterized as featuring computer technology and high-quality video graphics with the express intent of educating and entertaining their players (de Freitas, 2006; Squire, 2006). Serious educational games have proliferated, given funding agents' and educators' efforts to capitalize on the popularity of digital game play for classroom use. Specifically, the goal of these games is to promote transfer of learning and skills from game play to academic tasks. However, game development efforts often fail to adequately consider the cognitive sophistication or relative immaturity of its child and adolescent audience, and the appeal of these games compared to more recreational ones (Kato, 2012; Tüzün, 2007; Van Eck, 2006). (For exceptions, see Deater-Deckard, Chang, & Evans, and Revelle, this volume.)

We review here studies concerning the impact of games on cognitive skills, and children's and adolescents' perceptions of these games as learning tools. We conclude by discussing implications for future investigations of cognitive development in the context of video games.

Cognitive Skills Acquired During Recreational Video Game Play

Research on children and adolescents' cognition during game play has focused primarily on spatial skills and strategy use. This emphasis was reflected in the seminal 1994 volume of *Journal of Applied Developmental Psychology* (Volume 15) concerning the impact of video game play on late adolescents' and college-age students' cognitive abilities. For example, Subrahmanyam and Greenfield (1994) examined the extent to which playing a game that highlighted spatial skills, *Marble Madness*, enhanced 5th-graders' spatial ability. Findings showed improved spatial skill performance among those children who played the game relative to their counterparts who played a word game. The greatest improvement in spatial skills was found among those children who played *Marble Madness* and had showed relatively weak skills before playing.

Okagaki and Frensch (1994) showed that experience playing the video game *Tetris*, which highlights two-dimensional mental rotation and spatial visualization, resulted in improved performance on tasks assessing these skills among late adolescents. Their findings were confirmed by De Lisi and Wolford (2002), who had one group of 3rd-graders play *Tetris* and another play *Where in the USA Is Carmen Sandiego?*, which emphasizes social studies and geography content. Findings showed that, after repeated sessions playing one of the games, students who played *Tetris* showed significantly improved scores on a mental rotation skills task relative to their scores at the start of the sessions and relative to their peers who played *Where in the USA Is Carmen Sandiego?* Further, the former group's scores on the mental rotation task were correlated with their *Tetris* performance at the conclusion of the sessions. The authors concluded that because they played *Tetris* for several sessions, participants may have used similar solution strategies for the mental rotation task. Notably, before the *Tetris* game sessions, girls scored lower on the mental rotation task. However, after the sessions, boys and girls performed similarly on the task.

Game experience, whether naturalistic or provided in a given study, also provides a context for promoting reasoning and strategy use. For example, Fisch, Lesh, Motoki, Crespo, and Melfi (2011) found that 3rd- and 4th-graders showed improvements in mathematical reasoning skills and strategies after having played an online game emphasizing these skills. Researchers also have examined more general problem-solving strategies associated with game play. VanDeventer and White (2002) observed 10- and 11-year-old game players characterized as either highly or less highly skilled, as they taught "novice" or inexperienced adults to play *Super Mario Kart* and *Super Mario World*. During their instruction, highly skilled participants were more likely than less skilled participants to show evidence of planning, metacognition, awareness of how to circumvent obstacles, and opportunities to advance in the game. This pattern of findings parallels those found in the self-regulated learning literature (Zimmerman, 2008) and problem-solving literature (see Pirolli & Recker, 1995), in which greater evidence of managing one's learning results in better performance.

Hamlen (2011) has examined the strategies that 4th- and 5th-graders reported using to improve their performance on the games they frequently played. Interestingly, strategy use differed across gender, frequency of play, and game genre (e.g., action, adventure, educational, simulation). Girls were more likely than boys to use observation (e.g., watching others play), exploration (e.g., examining what actions work in the game), and innovation (e.g., thinking of new ways to solve the game) when playing games; boys were more likely to use cheat codes and ask friends for help. Frequent players were also more likely to use repetition (e.g., replaying the game) and cheat codes as strategies for game mastery. When playing action and educational games, boys were more likely than girls to use a repetition strategy. However, when playing adventure and simulation games, boys were more likely than girls to use a role-play strategy (i.e., imagine oneself in the game and what one would do in the situation). Girls, by comparison, were more likely to use an observation strategy when playing adventure games. Blumberg and Sokol (2004) also found that strategy use differed by frequency of play, as frequent 2nd- and 5th-grade players were more likely to report using internally based or self-reliant strategies such as trial and error to learn how to play a novel game. However, whereas Hamlen found that frequent players sought help and support for game play, Blumberg and Sokol found this approach among infrequent players only.

Developmental differences in strategy use also was found in research in which 5th- through 7th-graders were to think aloud as they negotiated a novel video game (see Blumberg, Altschuler, & Almonte, 2011; Blumberg & Ismailer, 2009). Surprisingly, these differences were not apparent for skills seen as exemplifying problem-solving behavior, such as reference to game strategies, insight, overarching goals and subgoals for game play, or acknowledgement of an impasse. Developmental differences were found as references to more short-term goals for game play or the completion of a specific subgoal decreased by grade and references to game progress increased by grade.

Collectively, the findings above demonstrate that frequency of play influences the strategies that children and adolescents report when asked about their game play. When prompted to spontaneously comment while instructing (i.e., as in VanDeventer & White, 2002) or playing, verbal protocols show greater evidence than survey responses of over-arching problem-solving behaviors children and adolescents use during game play and potentially, learning in general. Blumberg and colleagues' think-aloud findings (2011) suggest that these behaviors may not, in an obvious fashion, reflect differential game experience or levels of cognitive development. In their work, 5th- and 6th-graders showed greater evidence of behaviors exemplifying problem solving than 7th-graders. Given their presumed cognitive sophistication, one might have expected greater problem-solving behaviors among the 7th-graders. Further exploration of these findings may have entailed debriefing. Debriefing entails having players reflect on their game play and how their experiences apply outside the game (Crookall, 2010) and has been linked to transfer of learning in the gaming and educational technology literature (Crookall, 2010; de Freitas, 2006). Debriefing has yet to be used to elicit children's and adolescents' impressions of their cognition during game play. However, a recent line of research has emerged that directly examines their perspectives about the benefit of video games for classroom learning. Potentially, these impressions, as those provided via debriefing, have ramifications for transfer of learning from game play to academic tasks. We present studies from this line below.

Children's and Adolescents' Conceptions of Video Game Play

Research concerning children's and adolescents' reflections on what it is that they like about video game play and how they view their learning within it are sparse despite the value of the content to be gained for developing appealing educational games. Hamlen's study (2011) is among the few. As part of her examination of children's video game strategies, Hamlen (2011) asked her 4th- and 5th-grade participants what they liked about video games. More than 80% of the 118 students reported reasons for playing that did not pertain to specific characteristics of a given game. For example, 26% of the participants reported that they liked games given their interest in games in general, 14% reported that games provided freedom from real-world restrictions, and 13% appreciated the challenge within games. According to Hamlen, children viewed video games as presenting challenges without negative repercussions.

Bourgonjon, Valcke, Soetaert, and Schellens (2010) focused directly on students' views of video games as integral to classroom learning. Specifically, they queried Flemish secondary students aged 12–20 about their preference for video games as part of classroom activities and their perceptions of that potential incorporation as benefiting their learning. Findings showed that all students' perceptions of gaming and its academic value were moderated by their comfort with gaming and belief in its academic value, which in turn were influenced by students' game experience. Gender differences were found, as females were less inclined than males to favor video games in the classroom, although they were as likely as males to believe that games provided venues for learning. Females' lack of preference for video games may have reflected their less frequent video game experience as compared with the males.

We also explored children and adolescents' views of video game learning and its similarities to and differences from classroom learning in focus groups of 4th- through 8th-graders (Blumberg et al., 2011). For each grade, one or two groups of frequent video game players (those who play three or more times per week) and one of infrequent players (those who play two or fewer times per week), with the exception of 6th grade, were convened. Groups ranged from four to six students and included comparable numbers of males and females when possible. A total of 44 frequent and 24 infrequent players participated. The focus groups explored questions such as: 1) What do you like most about playing video games?; 2) What do you do when you're first learning how to play a video game?; 3) What happens when you get stuck in a video game?; 4) What happens when you get stuck on a problem in school?; and 5) How are problems in video games similar to/different from problems in schoolwork?

All students viewed video game play as opportunities for mastery and entertainment. Further, all students noted trial and error as their primary strategy for video game play, differing from that reported by Blumberg and Sokol (2004), who found trial and error strategies noted among frequent players only. When asked about their approaches to resolving impasses encountered in video game play and in school, all students noted seeking help, although frequent players identified more sources for both the video game and school contexts than the infrequent players. These sources included consulting manuals and textbooks, and asking teachers and friends.

Because of educators' keen interest in using digital games to promote learning, we asked participants how they viewed similarities and differences between school learning and video game play. All students generally saw both video game play and school learning as educational in nature. The 8th-graders in particular noted that both types of learning required practice. When asked to distinguish school learning from video game play, all 4th- and 5th-graders noted the lack of consequences attached to video game actions. Specifically, they noted the low stakes nature of video game play, in which behaviors were ungraded, mistakes went unpenalized, and teachers were not evaluating them. All 7th-graders commented that game play, rather than school work, provided choices in the type of tasks they could pursue, and the ability to control the pace and level of difficulty. Overall, students viewed learning as integral to game play and school activities. However, school learning was seen as having higher stakes and video game learning as allowing more personal control.

Collectively, the findings reviewed above elucidate children and adolescents' perceptions of learning in the video game and school context. Further information remains to be gleaned, potentially in the context of studies that entail debriefing, about how these perceptions inform the learning transferred across the two settings.

Conclusions

As noted earlier, promotion of video game play as an academic learning tool largely stems from educators' and funding agents' efforts to capitalize on game play appeal and reported cognitive benefits. However, the expectations for transfer of learning across game and learning contexts that are yielded via educational games may warrant tempering. Findings suggest that transfer from game play to more academic tasks, regardless of age, may be limited. For example, Sims and Mayer (2002) found that young adults' experience playing *Tetris* facilitated performance on mental rotation tasks only when *Tetris*-like shapes were used. In one of the few studies to examine adolescents, Masson, Bub, and Lalonde (2011) found that middle school students' conceptualizations about the trajectories of objects in motion improved after playing a game in which these trajectories could be manipulated rather than a strategy game. However, students' learning about objects in motion was limited to a general understanding of the shape of trajectories.

Whether transfer of learning always will be limited among child and adolescent samples clearly warrants greater consideration. For example, Fisch's work (see this volume) demonstrates transfer of content across learning tasks and diverse media platforms. Investigation of children's and adolescents' cognitive development in the ecologies in which they are now based, which include digital media in general and video games in particular, should be on the agenda of developmental psychologists. If our goal is to understand children's and adolescents' cognitive development as impacted by their daily experience, it's time we got into the game.

References

Blumberg, F. C. (2011). Introduction to special section: Ramifications of video game play for academic learning and cognitive skill acquisition. *Child Development Perspectives*, 5(2), 73–74. doi:10.1111/j.1750-8606.2011.00158.x

Blumberg, F. C., Altschuler, E. A., & Almonte, D. E. (2011, March). Children's perceptions of learning in videogames and school. In F. C. Blumberg & S. M. Fisch (Co-chairs), *Children's learning in videogame and academic settings*. Symposium conducted at Society for Research in Child Development Meeting, Montreal, Canada.

Blumberg, F. C., & Ismailer, S. S. (2009). What do children learn from playing video games? In U. Ritterfeld, M. Cody, & P. Vorderer (Eds.), *Serious games: Mechanisms and effects* (pp. 131–121). New York, NY: Routledge, Taylor, and Francis.

Blumberg, F. C., & Sokol, L. M. (2004). Boys' and girls' use of cognitive strategy when learning to play video games. *Journal of General Psychology, 131*(2), 151–158. doi:10.3200/GENP.131.2.151-158

Boot, W. R., Kramer, A. F., Simons, D. J., Fabiani, M., & Gratton, G. (2008). The effects of video game playing on attention, memory, and executive control. *Acta Psychologica, 129*, 387–398. doi:10.1016/j.actpsy.2008.09.005

Bourgonjon, J., Valcke, M., Soetaert, R., & Schellens, T. (2010). Students' perceptions about the use of video games in the classroom. *Computers & Education, 54*, 1145–1156.

Crookall, D. (2010). Serious games, debriefing, and simulation/gaming as a discipline. *Simulation & Gaming, 41*, 898–920. doi:10.1177/1046878110390784

de Freitas, S. (2006). Using games and simulations for supporting learning. *Learning, Media and Technology, 31*, 343–358.

De Lisi, R., & Wolford, J. L. (2002). Improving children's mental rotation accuracy with computer game playing. *The Journal of Genetic Psychology, 163*(3), 272–282. doi:10.1080/00221320209598683

Entertainment Software Association. (2012). 2012 essential facts about the computer and video game industry. Retrieved July 01, 2012, from www.theesa.com/facts/pdfs/ESA_EF_2012.pdf

Ferguson, C. J. (2010). Blazing angels or resident evil? Can violent video games be a force for good? *Review of General Psychology, 14*(2), 68–81. doi:10.1037/a0018941

Fisch, S. M., Lesh, R., Motoki, E., Crespo, S., & Melfi, V. (2011). Children's mathematical reasoning in online games: Can data mining reveal strategic thinking? *Child Development Perspectives, 5*(2), 88–92. doi:10.1111/j.1750-8606.2011.00161.x

Gee, J. P. (2003). *What video games have to teach us about learning and literacy*. New York, NY: Palgrave Macmillan.

Green, C. S., & Bavelier, D. (2003). Action video game modifies visual selective attention. *Nature, 423*(6939), 534–538. doi:10.1038/nature01647

Green, C. S., & Bavelier, D. (2006a). Effect of action video games on spatial distribution of visuospatial attention. *Journal of Experimental Psychology: Human Perception and Performance, 32*(6), 1465–1478. doi:10.1037/0096-1523.32.6.1465

Green, C. S., & Bavelier, D. (2006b). Enumeration versus multiple object tracking: The case of action video game players. *Cognition, 101*(1), 217–245. doi:10.1016/j.cognition.2005.10.004

Green, C. S., & Bavelier, D. (2007). Action video game experience alters the spatial resolution of attention. *Psychological Science, 18*, 88–94. doi:10.1111/j.1467–9280.2007.01853.x

Greenfield, P. M. (1994). Video games as cultural artifacts. *Journal of Applied Developmental Psychology, 15*(1), 3–12. doi:10.1016/0193-3973(94)90003-5

Greenfield, P. M., Camaioni, L., Ercolani, P., Weiss, L., Lauber, B. A., & Perucchini, P. (1994). Cognitive socialization by computer games in two cultures: Inductive discovery or mastery of an iconic code? *Journal of Applied Developmental Psychology, 15*(1), 59–85. doi:10.1016/0193-3973(94)90006-X

Hamlen, K. R. (2011). Children's choices and strategies in video games. *Computers in Human Behavior, 27*(1), 532–539. doi:10.1016/j.chb.2010.10.001

Karle, J. W., Watter, S., & Shedden, J. M. (2010). Task switching in video game players: Benefits of selective attention but not resistance to proactive interference. *Acta Psychologica, 134*(1), 70–78. doi:10.1016/j.actpsy.2009.12.007

Kato, P. M. (2012). Evaluating efficacy and validating games for health. *Games for Health Journal: Research, Development, and Clinical Applications, 1*(1), 74–76.

Lehrman, R. A. (2012, March 18). Video game nation: Why so many play. *Christian Science Monitor.* Retrieved July 9, 2012, from www.csmonitor.com/USA/Society/2012/0318/Video-game-nation-Why-so-many-play

MacArthur Foundation Digital Media Digital Learning Initiative. (2012, September). *Digital Media and Learning.* Retrieved from www.macfound.org/media/article_pdfs/Digital_Media_Learning_Info_Sheet.pdf

Masson, M. E. J., Bub, D. N., & Lalonde, C. E. (2011). Video-game training and naïve reasoning about object motion. *Applied Cognitive Psychology, 25*(1), 166–173. doi:10.1002/acp.1658

Okagaki, L., & Frensch, P. (1994). Effects of video game playing on measures of spatial performance: Gender effects in late adolescence. *Journal of Applied Developmental Psychology, 15*(1), 33–58. doi:10.1016/0193-3973(94)90005-1

Pillay, H. (2002). An investigation of the cognitive processes engaged in by recreational computer game players: Implications for skills of the future. *Journal of Research on Technology in Education, 34,* 336–350.

Pirolli, P., & Recker, M. M. (1995). Modeling individual differences in students' learning strategies. *Journal of the Learning Sciences, 4,* 1–38.

Rideout, V. J., Foehr, U. G., & Roberts, D. F. (2010). *Generation M²: Media in the lives of 8- to 18-year-olds.* Menlo Park, CA: Kaiser Family Foundation.

Salonius-Pasternak, D. E., & Gelfond, H. S. (2005). The next level of research on electronic play: Potential benefits and contextual influences for children and adolescents. *Human Technology: An Interdisciplinary Journal on Humans in ICT Environments, 1,* 5–22.

Sims, V. K., & Mayer, R. E. (2002). Domain specificity of spatial expertise: The case of video game players. *Applied Cognitive Psychology, 16,* 97–115.

Squire, K. (2006). From content to context: Videogames as designed experience. *Educational Researcher, 35,* 19–29.

Squire, K. D. (2008). Video game–based learning: An emerging paradigm for instruction. *Performance Improvement Quarterly, 21*(2), 7–36. doi:10.1002/piq.20020

Staiano, A. E., Abraham, A. A., & Calvert, S. L. (2012). Competitive versus cooperative exergame play for African American adolescents' executive function skills: Short-term effects in a long-term training intervention. *Developmental Psychology, 48*(2), 337–342. doi:10.1037/a0026938

Subrahmanyam, K., & Greenfield, P. M. (1994). Effect of video game practice on spatial skills in girls and boys. *Journal of Applied Developmental Psychology, 15*(1), 13–32. doi:10.1016/0193-3973(94)90004-3

Tüzün, H. (2007). Blending video games with learning: Issues and challenges with classroom implementations in the Turkish context. *British Journal of Educational Technology, 38,* 465–477.

VanDeventer, S. S., & White, J. A. (2002). Expert behavior in children's video game play. *Simulation & Gaming, 33,* 28–48.

Van Eck, R. V. (2006). Digital game–based learning. *Educause Review, 41*(2), 17–30.

Zimmerman, B. J. (2008). Investigating self-regulation and motivation: Historical background, methodological developments, and future prospects. *American Educational Research Journal, 45*(1), 166–183. doi:10.3102/0002831207312909

EDUCATION LIBRARY
UNIVERSITY OF KENTUCKY

FRAN C. BLUMBERG *is an associate professor, Division of Psychological & Educational Services, Fordham University Graduate School of Education, New York, USA, and can be reached via e-mail at blumberg@fordham.edu.*

ELIZABETH A. ALTSCHULER *is a doctoral student in counseling psychology, Fordham University Graduate School of Education, New York, USA, and can be reached via e-mail at ealtschuler@fordham.edu.*

DEBBY E. ALMONTE *is a doctoral student in educational psychology, Fordham University Graduate School of Education, New York, USA, and can be reached via e-mail at dalmonte@fordham.edu.*

MAXWELL I. MILEAF *is a master's student in counseling psychology, Fordham University Graduate School of Education, New York, USA, and can be reached via e-mail at itsmaxmileaf@gmail.com.*

NEW DIRECTIONS FOR CHILD AND ADOLESCENT DEVELOPMENT • DOI: 10.1002/cad

Calvert, S. L., Staiano, A. E., & Bond, B. J. (2013). Electronic gaming and the obesity crisis. In F. C. Blumberg & S. M. Fisch (Eds.), *Digital Games: A Context for Cognitive Development. New Directions for Child and Adolescent Development, 139,* 51–57.

6

Electronic Gaming and the Obesity Crisis

Sandra L. Calvert, Amanda E. Staiano, Bradley J. Bond

Abstract

Children and adolescents in the United States and in many countries are projected to have shorter life spans than their parents, partly because of the obesity crisis engulfing the developed world. Exposure to electronic media is often implicated in this crisis because media use, including electronic game play, may promote sedentary behavior and increase consumption of high-calorie foods and beverages that are low in nutritional value. Electronic games, however, may increase children's physical activity and expose them to healthier foods. We examine the role of electronic games in the pediatric obesity crisis and their contribution to more favorable health outcomes. © 2013 Wiley Periodicals, Inc.

In just three short decades, the U.S. pediatric obesity rate has tripled (McGinnis, Gootman, Kraak, & the Committee on Food Marketing and the Diets of Children and Youth, 2006); the percentage of 6- to 11-year-old children who were obese increased from 7% in 1980 to 20% in 2008 (Ogden, Carroll, Curtin, Lamb, & Flegal, 2010). The escalating obesity rates are not likely caused by genetic factors alone in such a short time frame, implicating the environment as a major contributor to this health crisis.

Maintaining the same weight involves energy balance, in which the number of calories consumed is equal to the number of calories expended (Calvert, 2008). Two environmental factors that have been implicated as causing obesity involve the consumption of high-fat, low-nutrient foods and beverages, and the sedentary life style that is now common in our nation from watching so much television or playing sedentary video games (Vandewater & Cummings, 2008). Media exposure, particularly to television advertising, has been linked to childhood food preferences and consumption of high-fat, low-nutrient foods (McGinnis et al., 2006). The link between media exposure and sedentary behavior, however, has been more difficult to demonstrate, particularly since media are increasingly mobile as youth move (e.g., walk and talk) when using them. For example, children can work out while listening to their iPods or move while interacting with exergames, which are video games that require gross motor movement for game play (Staiano & Calvert, 2011a).

Like food and beverage diets, then, media use also involves a diet comprised of activities that can potentially increase or decrease caloric balance. Put another way, the quality of media exposure as well as the quantity of media exposure should be considered given that U.S. 8- to 18-year-olds play electronic games for an average of 90 minutes per day (Rideout, Foehr, & Roberts, 2010). Our goal here is to describe how we can put those 90 minutes to good use so that we can alter the course of the pediatric obesity crisis.

Food and Beverage Marketing to Children

Media provide platforms for marketers of low-nutrient foods to reach children and adolescents, which can increase obesity and other health-related issues such as type II diabetes and cardiovascular disease (Calvert, 2008). After examining the extant literature, a National Academies Committee concluded that there were causal links between food and beverage advertising and children's food preferences, their food choices, and their short-term food consumption, as well as correlational links with adiposity (i.e., body fatness) (McGinnis et al., 2006). At that time, the literature consisted almost entirely of television advertising studies. An emerging, but neglected, area of research involves online marketing.

Subsequent research in the online marketing world revealed that similar kinds of products and techniques were used to market to children in the online and television spheres. For instance, an examination of the top 10 websites visited by 8- to 11-year-old children found that 70% of these sites marketed food to children, primarily candy, cereal, quick-serve restaurants, and snacks, and advergames were used to market products on some of these sites (Alvy & Calvert, 2008). Consistent with these findings, content analyses of food websites found that marketing unhealthy foods was pervasive (Moore, 2006; Weber, Story, & Harnack, 2006), with techniques like advergames being used to engage children in marketed content in game-like contexts (Moore, 2006).

Though far less prevalent, the same techniques used to make interacting with online food sites fun for children can also be used to market healthier foods and beverages. Dole Food Company, Inc., offers one such example. Using one of the Dole advergames as a guide, Pempek and Calvert (2009) created an advergame based on PAC-MAN® that rewarded consumption of healthy products such as orange juice, bananas, apples, and carrots, while punishing the consumption of unhealthy products such as soda, chips, and cookies. In another condition, the reward contingencies were reversed so that children were rewarded for consumption of the unhealthy products and punished for the consumption of the healthy ones. After 3rd- and 4th-grade low-income children played the advergame for 10 minutes, they selected and ate a snack. There was also a control condition where children selected the snack first and then played the advergame. Children who played the healthier version of the advergame selected and consumed more healthy snacks than those in the unhealthy advergame condition, with the control group falling in the middle of these two groups.

In a naturalistic study involving online advergames that promoted healthy or unhealthy foods, Harris, Speers, Schwartz, and Brownell (2012) found that 1.2 million children visited food company websites each month, and they devoted about 1 hour of their time on some of these websites. Children comprised more of the visitors on websites with advergames. These sites primarily promoted candy, sugared cereals, and fast food that involve heavy concentrations of calories, which, if consumed, would increase the likelihood of weight gain. When 7- to 12-year-old children played advergames that promoted unhealthy foods from these websites, they were more likely to subsequently consume snacks that were poor in nutritional value. Results were stronger for those who had played advergames in the past. By contrast, when they played advergames that promoted healthy foods, children were more likely to consume fruits and vegetables. However, only one website (once again, Dole) promoted healthy foods via advergames (Harris et al., 2012). Taken together, the results suggest that children will eat and consume the kinds of products that are marketed via advergames to them, be they healthy or unhealthy foods. Notably, marketers overwhelmingly promote unhealthy foods.

Food Preferences and Mobile Apps

Another approach to get children to eat healthy is via mobile phone apps. For example, *Time to Eat* is an app in which a virtual pet gives grade school–aged children feedback about their breakfast consumption. Eating breakfast is associated with lower, more healthy weights, whereas children who skip breakfast eat more poorly and have higher, less healthy weights (Sjoberg, Hallberg, Hoglund, & Hulthen, 2003). Byrne and colleagues (2012) provided motivational incentives for children to eat breakfast through virtual pets who provided feedback to children after they sent pictures of their breakfasts to their pets via their mobile phones. Children whose pets looked happy and sad were twice as likely to eat breakfast as those who only got happy feedback from their virtual pets or those who had no virtual pet at all. Those whose pets looked sad as well as happy were also more likely to report feeling attached to their pet than those who only received positive feedback from their pet. The implication of this study is that a combination of positive and negative feedback from virtual pets can motivate children to eat breakfast, thereby getting their day off to a healthy start.

Movement, or the Lack Thereof, and Media Exposure

The sedentary behavior involved in consuming traditional media, including traditional video game play, is known as the displacement effect because media use is thought to displace more active physical experiences (see Vandewater & Cummings, 2008). However, links between television viewing or video game use with children's physical activities yield either small correlations or none whatsoever (Vandewater & Cummings, 2008). Instead, media use like television viewing seems to displace other indoor activities, such as board games, rather than vigorous outdoor activities that yield high levels of energy expenditure (Vandewater, Bickham, & Lee, 2006).

Moreover, not all screen exposure is created equally in terms of physical movement. For instance, sedentary video game play involves more caloric expenditure than television viewing (Wang & Perry, 2006). Even so, the findings are mixed, as 9- to 12-year-old girls who played moderate amounts of video games showed increased weight (Vandewater, Shim, & Caplovitz, 2004).

A recent game changer involves exergames, in which children engage in gross motor activity during game play (Staiano & Calvert, 2011a), an experience that results in caloric expenditure (Graf, Pratt, Hester, & Short, 2009). Exergame play results in more energy expenditure than sedentary video game play (Graves, Stratton, Ridgers, & Cable, 2007), yielding about as much caloric expenditure as walking at a 3-mile-per-hour pace (Bausch, Beran, Cahanes, & Krug, 2008).

Social variables play an important role when examining the impact of exergame play, particularly during adolescence. For instance, African American adolescents who played Wii tennis in a short-term competitive situation expended more calories than those who played alone (Staiano & Calvert, 2011b). In a follow-up longitudinal study of overweight and obese African American adolescents that lasted 6 months, however, competitive exergame play did not yield weight loss, but cooperative exergame play did (Staiano, Abraham, & Calvert, 2012). More specifically, youth who played Wii Active exergames in rotating teams with the goal of losing the most calories on a weekly basis lost weight when compared to a no-treatment control group as well as to their own baseline scores. By contrast, those who competed as individuals in teams to lose the most weight stayed at about their same baseline weights.

Social influence has also been examined through sensor-based monitoring with systems that involve gaming elements. Examples of these systems include Chick Clique, Fish'n'Steps, and Shakra. Chick Clique and Fish'n'Steps both recorded step count from a pedometer, which was then shared across a social network of other users. Chick Clique automatically transmitted the user's step count to peers who were also playing the game. The competitive nature of the game resulted in an increase in the number of steps taken among high school students, but was unsuccessful in maintaining the interest of younger adolescents (Toscos, Faber, An, & Gandhi, 2006). In Fish'n'Steps, the number of steps taken contributed to visual feedback in the form of a fish that appeared in a fishbowl on a computer screen. Participants' fish were either represented in their own fish bowl (a solitary play condition) or in a communal fish tank with other users' fish (a cooperative yet competitive condition). Users in the cooperative condition reported that their influence on their peers' fish motivated them to keep their step count high during the day which, in turn, kept their fish healthy and happy (Lin, Mamykina, Lindtner, Delajoux, & Strub, 2006).

Mobile phones also play a key role in making sensor-based experiences enjoyable and motivating for the user. Shakra, for example, used mobile phone signals to determine the distance traveled and velocity, enabling differentiation among types of activity, such as running versus walking (Anderson et al., 2007). This kind of information can also be applied to competitive mobile game applications. For example, Fujiki, Kazakos, Puri, Buddharaju, and Pavlidis (2008) developed an innovative sensor-based application that ran in the background of a mobile phone at all times. Every movement counted toward the user's ultimate goal of winning a race against another user. The competitive nature of the race resulted in sustained motivation for the users to continue being physically active.

Taken together, the results from these studies suggest that exergames and mobile games have untapped promise to get youth to exercise and even lose weight. To be effective, social variables must be considered in order to sustain the kinds of activity levels that are necessary for beneficial health outcomes over the long run.

Conclusions

Energy balance, in terms of consuming the right kinds of media to promote healthy eating as well as physical movement, is within our grasp. Youth enjoy playing games, and the knowledge base is emerging to increase energy expenditure during exergames and mobile games as well as guide food consumption patterns via advergames and mobile games. Social variables, including cooperation and, to a certain extent, competition, as well as contingent feedback in terms of reinforcers, are key to effective behavioral changes. The challenge for us is to take the necessary steps as individuals and as a nation to tip the balance toward a healthier food and media environment for our children.

References

Alvy, E., & Calvert, S. L. (2008). Food marketing on popular children's websites: A content analysis. *Journal of the American Dietetic Association, 108,* 710–713.

Anderson, I., Maitland, J., Sherwood, S., Barkhuus, L., Chalmers, M., Hall, M., . . . Muller, H. (2007). Shakra: Tracking and sharing daily activity levels with unaugmented mobile phones. *Mobile Network Applications, 12,* 185–199.

Bausch, L., Beran, J., Cahanes, S., & Krug, L. (2008). Physiological responses while playing Nintendo Wii sports. *Journal of Undergraduate Kinesiology Research, 3,* 19–25.

Byrne, S., Gay, G. K., Pollak, J. P., Gonzales, A. L., Retelny, D., Lee, T., & Wansink, B. (2012). Caring for mobile phone–based virtual pets can influence youth eating behaviors. *Journal of Children and Media, 6,* 83–99.

Calvert, S. L. (2008). Children as consumers: Advertising and marketing. *The Future of Children, 18*(1), 205–234.

Fujiki, Y., Kazakos, K., Puri, C., Buddharaju, P., & Pavlidis, I. (2008). NEAT-o-Games: Blending physical activity and fun in the daily routine. *ACM Computers in Entertainment, 6*(2), 21:1–21:22. doi:10.1145/1371216.1371224

Graf, D., Pratt, L., Hester, C., & Short, K. (2009). Playing active video games increases energy expenditure in children. *Pediatrics, 124,* 534–540.

Graves, L., Stratton, G., Ridgers, N., & Cable, N. (2007). Comparison of energy expenditure in adolescents when playing new generation and sedentary computer games: Cross sectional study. *British Medical Journal, 335,* 1282–1284.

Harris, J., Speers, S., Schwartz, M., & Brownell, K. (2012). U.S. food company branded advergames on the Internet: Children's exposure and effects on snack consumption. *Journal of Children and the Media, 6,* 51–66.

Lin, J., Mamykina, L., Lindtner, S., Delajoux, G., & Strub, H. (2006). Fish'n'Steps: Encouraging physical activity with an interactive computer game. In *Proceedings of the 8th International Conference on Ubiquitous Computing (UbiComp'06),* Springer-Verlag: Berlin.Heidelberg, 261–278.

McGinnis, J. M., Gootman, J. A., Kraak, V. I. (Eds.), and the Committee on Food Marketing and the Diets of Children and Youth. (2006). *Food marketing to children and youth: Threat or opportunity?* Washington, DC: The National Academies Press.

Moore, E. (2006). *It's child's play: Advergaming and the online food marketing to children.* Menlo Park, CA: Kaiser Family Foundation.

Ogden, C. L., Carroll, M. D., Curtin, L. R., Lamb, M. M., & Flegal, K. M. (2010). Prevalence of high body mass index in U.S. children and adolescents, 2007–2008. *Journal of the American Medical Association, 303*, 242–249.

Pempek, T., & Calvert, S. L. (2009). Use of advergames to promote consumption of nutritious foods and beverages by low-income African American children. *Archives of Pediatrics and Adolescent Medicine, 163*(7), 633–637.

Rideout, V., Foehr, U., & Roberts, D. (2010). *Generation M^2: Media in the lives of 8- to 18-year-olds*. Menlo Park, CA: Kaiser Family Foundation.

Sjoberg, A., Hallberg, L., Hoglund, D., & Hulthen, L. (2003). Meal pattern, food choice, nutrient intake, and lifestyle factors in the Goteborg Adolescence Study. *European Journal of Clinical Nutrition, 57*, 1569–1578.

Staiano, A. E., Abraham, A. A., & Calvert, S. L. (2012). Adolescent exergame play for weight loss and psychosocial improvement: A controlled physical activity intervention. *Obesity*. Advance online publication. doi:10.1038/oby.2012.143

Staiano, A. E., & Calvert, S. L. (2011a). Exergames for physical education courses: Physical, social, and cognitive benefits. *Child Development Perspectives, 5*, 93–98.

Staiano, A. E., & Calvert, S. L. (2011b). Wii tennis play as physical activity in low-income African American adolescents. *CyberPsychology, 5*(1).

Toscos, T., Faber, A., An, S., & Gandhi, M. P. (2006). Chick Clique: Persuasive technology to motivate teenage girls to exercise. In *Proceedings of CHI '06*, ACM Press, 1873–1878.

Vandewater, E., Bickham, D., & Lee, J. (2006). Time well spent? Relating media use to children's free-time activities. *Pediatrics, 101*, 497–504.

Vandewater, E. A., & Cummings, H. (2008). Media use and childhood obesity. In S. L. Calvert & B. J. Wilson (Eds.), *Handbook of children, media, and development* (pp. 355–380). Boston, MA: Wiley-Blackwell.

Vandewater, E. A., Shim, M., & Caplovitz, A. (2004). Linking obesity and activity level with children's television and videogame use. *Journal of Adolescence, 27*, 71–85.

Wang, X., & Perry, A. (2006). Metabolic and physiologic responses to video game play in 7- to 10-year-old boys. *Archives of Pediatric and Adolescent Medicine, 160*, 411–415.

Weber, K., Story, M., & Harnack, L. (2006). Internet food marketing strategies aimed at children and adolescents: A content analysis of food and beverage brand web sites. *Journal of the American Dietetic Association, 106*(9), 1463–1466.

SANDRA L. CALVERT *is professor and director of the Children's Digital Media Center, Georgetown University, Washington DC, USA, and can be reached via e-mail at calvertsl@gmail.com.*

AMANDA E. STAIANO *is a postdoctoral research fellow at Pennington Biomedical Research Center, Baton Rouge, LA, USA, and can be reached via e-mail at amanda.staiano@pbrc.edu.*

BRADLEY J. BOND *is an assistant professor of communication at the University of San Diego, San Diego, CA, USA, and can be reached via e-mail at bradleybond@gmail.com.*

Fisch, S. M. (2013). Cross-platform learning: On the nature of children's learning from multiple media platforms. In F. C. Blumberg & S. M. Fisch (Eds.), *Digital Games: A Context for Cognitive Development. New Directions for Child and Adolescent Development, 139,* 59–70.

7

Cross-Platform Learning: On the Nature of Children's Learning from Multiple Media Platforms

Shalom M. Fisch

Abstract

It is increasingly common for an educational media project to span several media platforms (e.g., TV, Web, hands-on materials), assuming that the benefits of learning from multiple media extend beyond those gained from one medium alone. Yet research typically has investigated learning from a single medium in isolation. This paper reviews several recent studies to explore cross-platform learning (i.e., learning from combined use of multiple media platforms) and how such learning compares to learning from one medium. The paper discusses unique benefits of cross-platform learning, a theoretical mechanism to explain how these benefits might arise, and questions for future research in this emerging field. © 2013 Wiley Periodicals, Inc.

Many studies have demonstrated that children learn from watching well-designed educational television programs. Viewing of educational television has been found to contribute to children's knowledge, skills, and attitudes regarding subjects such as literacy, math, and science. The evidence regarding learning outcomes from interactive games is less extensive, but studies have found evidence of learning from interactive games as well. (For reviews, see Fisch, 2004, 2009; Honey & Hilton, 2012; Kirkorian & Anderson, 2011.)

Often, however, producers do not create "just" a television series. Amid industry buzzwords such as *multiplatform* and *transmedia*, it is increasingly common for projects to span several media platforms, so that an educational television series might be accompanied by a related website, hands-on outreach materials, museum exhibit, or live show. From an educational standpoint, producers and funders assume this combination of media yields added benefits for children's learning beyond those that might be provided by one medium alone.

But is this assumption true? Until recently, research has focused almost entirely on the impact of one media component in isolation, such as a television series or a computer game, not a set of components that span multiple platforms. The lack of research on learning from multiple media—what my colleagues and I refer to as *cross-platform learning* (Fisch, Lesh, Motoki, Crespo, & Melfi, in press)—leaves open important questions such as: How does learning from multiple media platforms compare to learning from a single medium? By what mechanisms does such learning occur?

This paper reviews several recent studies that compared learning from a single medium to learning from cumulative use of multiple related media. Data from these studies will be used to draw inferences about the nature and benefits of cross-platform learning—that is, the potential synergy among related media components and how they might interact to yield cumulative educational outcomes.

Empirical Research

The foundation for the present discussion stems from three evaluations of children's learning from educational media. These studies, respectively, investigated learning from the following multiple-media projects for informal education:

- *Panwapa*, a multiple-media project for 4- to 7-year-olds, that was designed to promote positive attitudes, skills, and behavior regarding several aspects of global citizenship (e.g., awareness of the wider world, appreciating similarities and differences, and understanding and being responsive to economic disparity). *Panwapa* was distributed

NEW DIRECTIONS FOR CHILD AND ADOLESCENT DEVELOPMENT • DOI: 10.1002/cad

internationally in several languages. Its components included a set of videos, a website in which children could play games and create a web page to describe themselves (and visit pages created by children in other countries), and hands-on activities for classroom use. Research examined pretest–posttest gains in four countries, with children in each country assigned to one of three treatment groups; one group was assigned to use *Panwapa* videos and hands-on activities for four weeks, a second group used these materials plus the website, and a third (control) group used none of the materials (Fisch et al., 2010).

- *Between the Lions*, a children's television program for 4- to 7-year-olds, accompanied by hands-on ancillary materials, designed to support early literacy development. Research compared pre–post growth among children who viewed abridged videos of the television series, either with or without reinforcement from accompanying hands-on classroom materials. To investigate the potential role that characters might play in facilitating cross-platform effects, children used hands-on materials that did or did not incorporate characters from the *Between the Lions* videos. A control group did not use any of the videos or hands-on materials (Piotrowski, Jennings, & Linebarger, in press).

- *Cyberchase*, a multiple-media project that promoted mathematical problem solving and positive attitudes toward mathematics among 8- to 11-year-olds. The *Cyberchase* components included an animated television series, a website with interactive games and puzzles, and hands-on games and activities for classroom use. Research compared pre–post change in mathematical problem solving between children who were assigned to either view *Cyberchase* videos, play games on the *Cyberchase* website, use both of these media, or use both media plus hands-on classroom activities (Fisch et al., in press).

All three studies produced patterns of data that were consistent both with each other and with past research on the impact of educational media. As in prior research, all three studies found that educational media users showed significant pretest–posttest growth in their understanding of educational content as compared to the control groups that did not use the materials. (Notably, the effects of *Between the Lions* were not as strong as in prior studies of the series' impact, perhaps because Piotrowski and her colleagues employed abridged, rather than full, episodes of the television series, or perhaps because the children in their sample entered the study with stronger pre-existing literacy skills than in previous research; cf Linebarger, Kosanic, Greenwood, & Doku, 2004; Linebarger & McMenamin, 2010.)

Beyond the basic impact of educational media, however, comparisons among the groups that used different combinations of materials revealed that, in all of these studies, some combinations of materials yielded more consistently significant educational outcomes than others. In the

Cyberchase study, effects were often stronger for the group that used both videos and online games than for groups that used either medium by itself. The *Panwapa* study yielded few significant differences in direct comparisons between the groups that used different combinations of *Panwapa* materials, but when each group was compared to the control group, significant effects emerged more often in the group that used all three types of materials (video, Web, and hands-on activities) than in the group that used the videos and hands-on materials without the website. Similarly, some measures in the *Between the Lions* research indicated that kindergartners (but not younger children) who used video plus hands-on materials demonstrated greater literacy gains than those who used video alone. Thus, data from at least some measures in all three studies suggested that combined use of multiple media produced greater learning than use of a single medium alone. In other words, cross-platform learning produced stronger and/or more consistent outcomes than learning from individual media platforms in isolation.

However, none of the studies found that the strongest learning effects *always* emerged in the group that used the greatest number of media components. The strongest and most consistent effects in the *Cyberchase* study were found among children in the "DVD + Web" group, which used a combination of videos and online games, not the "All Materials" group, which used both of those components plus additional hands-on activities. In the *Panwapa* study, impact on some aspects of global citizenship (e.g., naming their own and other countries, awareness of other languages) was significant only among children who used all forms of *Panwapa* media. However, impact on other aspects (e.g., similarities and differences across cultures, differentiating between needs and wants) was significant among both the group that used all materials and the group that used videos and hands-on materials without the website; no significant difference emerged between the two groups (although both outperformed the control group). Similarly, the *Between the Lions* study found that on measures of more basic literacy skills (e.g., letter naming fluency), the addition of hands-on materials yielded stronger effects than viewing alone. However, on measures of more sophisticated skills (e.g., initial sound fluency, rhyme awareness), effects were stronger if children watched the series *without* hands-on activities, especially if the hands-on materials did not employ the characters seen in the *Between the Lions* videos.

Collectively, these findings suggest that, under some conditions, cross-platform learning produces stronger and more consistent learning outcomes than use of a single medium in isolation. However, in some cases, stronger effects may be found among groups that use fewer media components, indicating that it is not simply the case that "more is better" or that positive effects of cross-platform learning can be explained via the amount of time spent engaging with the embedded educational content. If either of these explanations were correct, effects would always be strongest (or at least equally strong) in the treatment group that uses the greatest number of media components. All three of the above studies demonstrate that is not the case.

How, then, can we explain the fact that, in many cases, cross-platform learning does produce greater outcomes? The results of these studies—both the successes and the failures of multiple media in eliciting enhanced learning effects—lend insight into unique benefits of cross-platform learning and likely mechanisms by which these benefits might arise.

Benefits for Comprehension and Learning

Some benefits of cross-platform learning can be attributed less to the unique nature of such learning per se and more to opportunities that arise from multiple presentations of related educational content and the use of more than one medium. Examples of these benefits include the ability to provide multiple entry points for children to engage with the educational content and the opportunity to match aspects of the educational content to the most appropriate media for their delivery. Others stem from the nature of cross-platform learning itself, which I attribute to transfer of learning, as discussed below.

Matching Content to the Most Appropriate Medium. Every medium carries its own affordances—that is, characteristics of the medium that make it particularly well suited to certain kinds of content (e.g., Rabinowitz, Blumberg, & Everson, 2004; cf. Norman, 1988). For example, interactive games are uniquely suited to providing contingent feedback and scaffolding, whereas television programs lend themselves well to embedding educational content in a compelling narrative or portraying documentary-style accounts of real-world applications of content.

Apart from the affordances that an entire medium provides on a broad level, the design of specific games or activities within a given medium also lend themselves to conveying particular aspects of educational content. The *Panwapa* website used the name of a child's home country as part of his or her login, and a clickable globe as one of the chief means of navigation when visiting other children's home pages. Thus, it is understandable that, in most cases, children who used the website (in combination with other media) showed significantly greater gains than the control group in naming their own and other countries, while children who used other *Panwapa* media without the website did not. Similarly, many of the significant effects regarding children's knowledge about languages were found among users of the website who had played an online hide-and-seek game about foreign languages (although some significant language effects appeared for those who used videos and hands-on activities too).

As this example illustrates, one advantage of multiple media over a single medium is that the use of multiple media presents producers with the flexibility to address various aspects of educational content via whichever media lend themselves best to conveying those aspects of the content.

Multiple Points of Entry. Even when the same or similar content is conveyed through the various components of a multiple-media project, a second advantage of such approaches lies in providing multiple entry points into that content. This can provide a useful means of reaching an individual child through the medium (or media) that he or she finds most appealing. The use of multiple media also accommodates a variety of learning styles or individual differences in preferred modes for learning (e.g., K. Dunn & R. Dunn, 1987; R. Dunn, Griggs, Olson, Beasley, & Gorman, 1995). If similar content is presented via several different kinds of media, visual learners (for example) can engage with the content via visual media, while learners who prefer verbal instruction can engage with the content via verbal media. Further, when educational media are designed for classroom or family use, multiple media also provide opportunities for adults to use the materials that are best suited to their schedules, available equipment, and/or educational philosophies.

Repetition and Reinforcement. In positing explanations for children's learning from the *Sesame Street* television series, Fisch and Truglio (2001) pointed to the value of its magazine format, in which each episode is comprised of a number of brief segments (animations, live-action sketches, etc.). Addressing a given concept in several different segments (e.g., a cluster of segments about the letter *B*) allows viewers multiple opportunities to practice and master the concept if they did not understand it fully the first time. In addition, presenting the same concept in multiple contexts (e.g., presenting and labeling *B* in the context of the words *bed*, *bath*, and *bird*) can encourage generalization of the concept. Because they have seen the concept at work in several different contexts, children may come to see the concept as applicable in many contexts, perhaps including contexts not presented on the screen. This concept, known as *varied practice* in the research literature on transfer of learning in education and problem solving, is seen as key in enabling learners to apply concepts to situations and contexts beyond the ones in which they were learned (e.g., Gick & Holyoak, 1983; Salomon & Perkins, 1989; Singley & Anderson, 1989).

The same idea can be applied across media, too. Just as a concept can be reinforced and expanded upon via multiple segments within a television program, the same concept (or related concepts) can be addressed in a television program, an interactive game, and a hands-on activity. These multiple engagements with the concept provide multiple opportunities for mastery and generalization. Moreover, given the point discussed above regarding affordances of various media, such engagements can build upon experiences that are well suited to each particular medium, such as an explanation and application of the concept in a television program, an opportunity to practice and work with the concept in an vo explanations highlight a key issue for multiple-media education: How much media is too much? Is there an opti-educational media use, beyond which—given children's cog-ty and/or the needs, constraints, and attitudes of adult -the benefits of cross-platform learning are diminished? Fur-will be needed to identify optimal approaches, with impor-ions for the design of educationally effective materials for n learning.

essential, but unanswered, question concerns developmental cross-platform learning. Some nonmedia studies of transfer n areas such as analogical reasoning and metaphor, have -lihood of transfer to increase with age (e.g., Brown, Kane, & entner, 1988), perhaps because older children can draw on a ledge base or because they are better able to appreciate lational structure instead of relying merely on surface fea-legree that the benefits of cross-platform learning stem from easonable to expect that older children may be better able to nt and skills across media, and thus benefit more from cross-ning. Indeed, Piotrowski and colleagues (in press) found ; of multiple media among 6-year-olds than 4-year-olds, h and colleagues (2010) found main effects of age (4 to 7 significant interactions between age and the impact of differ-ons of Panwapa materials. (Data from Fisch and colleagues' of Cyberchase do not directly address developmental issues, participating children were approximately the same age.) It hat different patterns of developmental differences might ng on factors such as the nature of the educational content ed or the number and types of media components used. ing studies have only begun to address this issue, so further ded to gain a greater understanding of ways in which devel-ts with characteristics of both materials and users to impact

tform learning is a newly emerging field, it is not surprising questions have yet to be answered. That said, the studies ate have already taken the essential first step of demonstrat-al of cross-platform approaches to promote learning out-those of a single medium. Moreover, transfer of learning vide a promising direction in explaining the mechanisms he effects of cross-platform learning, as children apply skills gained from one medium to produce richer engage-he process of learning from a second medium. As the media inues to move further in the direction of projects that

interactive game, and face-to-face support and scaffolding in a teacher-led hands-on activity.

Still, one medium can reinforce the lessons conveyed by another only if they share the same (or closely related) educational content. Thus, for such benefits to arise, educational content must be closely aligned across media. Further, parallel to Fisch and Truglio's (2001) observation about *Sesame Street*, children must *recognize* this alignment to draw the connec-tions necessary to gain the benefits of reinforcement across multiple media, as opposed to processing and learning from each experience in isolation.

Transfer of Learning as a Mechanism for Cross-Platform Learning

All three studies discussed earlier employed pre–post assessments whose tasks were different than those seen in the materials, although they reflected similar underlying educational content. Accordingly, the signifi-cant pretest–posttest effects in all three studies reflect *transfer of learning* (i.e., the learners' ability to apply concepts or skills acquired in one con-text to a new problem or context). Outside the realm of media, numerous theoretical mechanisms have been offered to explain how and when trans-fer of learning occurs in formal education and problem solving (e.g., Gentner, 1983; Greeno, Moore, & Smith, 1993; Holyoak, 1985; Salomon & Perkins, 1989; Schwartz, Bransford, & Sears, 2005). Elements of these approaches have been used to explain how transfer operates in informal education, such as educational television (Fisch, 2004).

However, data from the *Cyberchase* study also provided evidence of another form of transfer of learning—one that appears to lend insight into mechanisms at work in cross-platform learning. In this study, apart from the hands-on problem-solving assessments employed in the pretest and posttest, problem solving was also measured via online tracking data that recorded every mouse click while children played three *Cyberchase* online math games. Coding schemes used patterns of children's responses and errors to gain insight into the sophistication of the mathematical problem-solving strategies children used to play the games and the number of cor-rect answers they produced. (See Fisch, Lesh, Motoki, Crespo, & Melfi, 2011, for a detailed discussion of this methodology.)

Online tracking data were compared between the treatment group that only used the games and the group that used multiple *Cyberchase* media components. Children who used multiple media employed signifi-cantly more sophisticated mathematical strategies while playing the three online games (e.g., additive vs. simple matching strategies), and produced more correct responses while playing two of the three games. As in the posttest tasks, children appeared to take the educational content they encountered in one medium (television and/or hands-on activities) and apply it while engaging with math content in another medium (online games). Such transfer of learning supported their interaction with the second medium, allowing children to apply more sophisticated approaches and producing a richer, more successful engagement with the material.

This, I believe, is a unique, key characteristic of cross-platform learning: The lessons learned from one medium can be applied, not only to enhance children's general knowledge (as manifest in posttest assessments), but also to support and enrich children's experience *while they are in the process of learning from a second medium*. This richer engagement, coupled with the factors discussed earlier regarding multiple entry points and varied practice, results in the stronger pretest–posttest effects observed for cross-platform learning as compared to learning from a single medium.

Indeed, it is quite possible that cross-platform learning may not only provide opportunities for transfer of learning, but that the presence of the same characters and contexts across media may even facilitate such transfer. Research on transfer of learning has shown that it is more likely to occur when two situations appear similar on their face (*surface structure similarity*) than when they are dissimilar on their surface but rest on similar underlying principles (*deep structure similarity*; e.g., Bassok & Holyoak, 1993; Gentner & Forbus, 1991). Thus, encountering *Cyberchase* characters in an online game might lead children to think of other times when they saw the same characters (e.g., on television). This could facilitate the transfer of information and skills from one medium to another in a way that seeing different characters on television and in a game might not.

This hypothesis is supported by data from the *Between the Lions* study, in which children viewed *Between the Lions* videos either in isolation or with hands-on materials that either featured or did not feature illustrations of *Between the Lions* characters. The resulting effects did not attain statistical significance, but nonsignificant trends were found in the expected direction: Use of the videos plus hands-on materials with *Between the Lions* characters produced stronger gains in literacy than use of the videos alone. However, use of equivalent hands-on materials without *Between the Lions* characters did not produce such effects. (In fact, the impact of videos plus generic hands-on materials was actually smaller than that of videos alone.) As Fisch and Truglio (2001) would predict, the alignment between the educational content of the videos and hands-on materials was insufficient to produce greater learning by itself; rather, children had to recognize the connection between the two, and the presence of shared characters helped children make those connections.

Limitations of Cross-Platform Learning

If transfer across media is indeed a key mechanism at work in cross-platform learning, then factors that facilitate or inhibit transfer of learning

should operate similarly in facilitatin
ing. It is worth noting that, even in fo
mental settings, transfer of learning o
1993). To achieve successful transfer
tial presentation of content, create a
that is sufficiently abstract to extend l
tent was initially encountered, and re
new situation in which it might be
stages—such as a lack of initial con
that is too narrow or context-bound
application—would result in a failu
ford, Brown, & Cocking, 1999; Fisch

With that in mind, let us retur
reviewed above found that pretest–p
gest in the group that used the great
consider the explanations that the
Fisch and colleagues (2010) suggest
aspects of global citizenship appeare
groups used the components that a
For example, use of the website wa
ability to identify their own and oth
names were integral to children's lo
and her colleagues (in press) hypot
observed for *Between the Lions* coul
various literacy skills they assesse
participating children. For more l
learning appeared for kindergartne
because kindergartners were able
between the televised and hands-o
dren's limited cognitive capacity w
of televised and hands-on materia
the benefits of cross-platform lea
also pointed to the amount of *Cyl*
explain why effects were often st
games than for users of these me
addressing the amount of material
tive capacity, however, they raised
ers who were faced with the challe
their busy school day. Since this cl
classes used all of the materials, F
classes may not have used the ma
this treatment group may have
dissatisfaction.

It is difficult to know which
correct, or whether all of these fact

the latter
approaches
mal level of
nitive capa
gatekeepers
ther researc
tant implica
cross-platfo

Anothe
differences i
of learning,
found the li
Long, 1989;
greater kno
underlying
tures. To the
transfer, it is
transfer con
platform lea
greater effec
although Fis
years) but n
ent combina
in press stud
because all t
seems likely
arise, depend
being addres
However, exi
research is n
opment inter
on learning.

Conclusion

Since cross-p
that many ke
conducted to
ing the poter
comes beyon
appears to pr
that underlie
knowledge ar
ment while in
landscape co

employ multiple media platforms, future research will be invaluable both in helping us understand children's interactions with these media and in identifying ways in which such crossmedia approaches can be used most effectively for education.

References

Bassok, M., & Holyoak, K. J. (1993). Pragmatic knowledge and conceptual structure: Determinants of transfer across quantitative domains. In D. K. Detterman & R. J. Sternberg (Eds.), *Transfer on trial: Intelligence, cognition, and instruction* (pp. 68–98). Norwood, NJ: Ablex.

Bransford, J. D., Brown, A. L., & Cocking, R. R. (Eds.). (1999). *How people learn: Brain, mind, experience, and school.* Washington, DC: National Academy Press.

Brown, A. L., Kane, M. I., & Long, C. (1989). Analogical transfer in young children: Analogies as tools for communication and exposition. *Applied Cognitive Psychology, 3*, 275–293.

Detterman, D. K. (1993). The case for the prosecution: Transfer as an epiphenomenon. In D. K. Detterman & R. J. Sternberg (Eds.), *Transfer on trial: Intelligence, cognition, and instruction* (pp. 1–24). Norwood, NJ: Ablex.

Dunn, K., & Dunn, R. (1987). Disputing outmoded beliefs about student learning. *Educational Leadership, 44*(6), 55–62.

Dunn, R., Griggs, S. A., Olson, J., Beasley, M., & Gorman, B. S. (1995). A meta-analytic validation of the Dunn and Dunn model of learning-style preferences. *Journal of Educational Research, 88*, 353–362.

Fisch, S. M. (2004). *Children's learning from educational television: Sesame Street and beyond.* Mahwah, NJ: Lawrence Erlbaum.

Fisch, S. M. (2009). Educational television and interactive media for children: Effects on academic knowledge, skills, and attitudes. In J. Bryant & M. B. Oliver (Eds.), *Media effects: Advances in theory and research* (3rd ed.; pp. 402–435). New York, NY: Routledge.

Fisch, S. M., Hsueh, Y., Zhou, Z., Xu, C. J., Hamed, M., Khader, Z., . . . Guha, M. L. (2010). Crossing borders: Learning from educational media in four countries. *Televizion, 23*(1), 42–45.

Fisch, S. M., Lesh, R., Motoki, E., Crespo, S., & Melfi, V. (2011). Children's mathematical reasoning in online games: Can data mining reveal strategic thinking? *Child Development Perspectives, 5*, 88–92.

Fisch, S. M., Lesh, R., Motoki, E., Crespo, S., & Melfi, V. (in press). Cross-platform learning: How do children learn from multiple media? In F. C. Blumberg (Ed.), *Learning by playing: Frontiers of video gaming in education.* New York, NY: Oxford University Press.

Fisch, S. M., & Truglio, R. T. (2001). Why children learn from *Sesame Street.* In S. M. Fisch & R. T. Truglio (Eds.), *"G" is for growing: Thirty years of research on children and Sesame Street* (pp. 233–244). Mahwah, NJ: Lawrence Erlbaum Associates.

Gentner, D. (1983). Structure-mapping: A theoretical framework for analogy. *Cognitive Science, 7*, 155–170.

Gentner, D. (1988). Metaphor as structure mapping: The relational shift. *Child Development, 59*, 47–59.

Gentner, D., & Forbus, K. D. (1991). MAC/FAC: A model of similarity-based retrieval. *Cognitive Science, 19*, 141–205.

Gick, M. L., & Holyoak, K. J. (1983). Schema induction and analogical transfer. *Cognitive Psychology, 15*, 1–38.

Greeno, J. G., Moore, J. L., & Smith, D. R. (1993). Transfer of situated knowledge. In D. K. Detterman & R. J. Sternberg (Eds.), *Transfer on trial: Intelligence, cognition, and instruction* (pp. 99–167). Norwood, NJ: Ablex.

Holyoak, K. J. (1985). The pragmatics of analogical transfer. In G. H. Bower (Ed.), *The psychology of learning and motivation* (pp. 59–87). New York, NY: Academic Press.

Honey, M. A., & Hilton, M. L. (2012). *Learning science through computer games and simulations.* Washington, DC: National Academies Press.

Kirkorian, H. L., & Anderson, D. R. (2011). Learning from educational media. In S. L. Calvert & B. J. Wilson (Eds.), *The handbook of children, media, and development* (pp. 188–213). West Sussex, England: Wiley-Blackwell.

Linebarger, D. L., Kosanic, A. Z., Greenwood, C. R., & Doku, N. S. (2004). Effects of viewing the television program *Between the Lions* on the emergent literacy skills of young children. *Journal of Educational Psychology, 96*(2), 297–308.

Linebarger, D. L., & McMenamin, K. (2010). *Evaluation of the* Between the Lions *Mississippi literacy initiative, 2008–2009.* Philadelphia, PA: Annenberg School for Communication, University of Pennsylvania.

Norman, D. A. (1988). *The design of everyday things.* New York, NY: Basic Books.

Piotrowski, J. T., Jennings, N., & Linebarger, D. L. (in press). Extending the lessons of educational television with young American children. *Journal of Children and Media.*

Rabinowitz, M., Blumberg, F. C., & Everson, H. T. (Eds.). (2004). *The design of instruction and evaluation: Affordances of using media and technology.* Mahwah, NJ: Lawrence Erlbaum Associates.

Salomon, G., & Perkins, D. N. (1989). Rocky roads to transfer: Rethinking mechanisms of a neglected phenomenon. *Educational Psychologist, 24*(2), 113–142.

Schwartz, D. L., Bransford, J. D., & Sears, D. L. (2005). Efficiency and innovation in transfer. In J. Mestre (Ed.), *Transfer of learning from a modern multidisciplinary perspective* (pp. 1–51). Greenwich, CT: Information Age Publishing.

Singley, M. K., & Anderson, J. R. (1989). *The transfer of cognitive skill.* Cambridge, MA: Harvard University Press.

SHALOM M. FISCH is president and founder of MediaKidz Research & Consulting, New Jersey, USA, and can be reached via e-mail at mediakidz@lycos.com.

Levine, M. H., & Vaala, S. E. (2013). Games for learning: Vast wasteland or a digital promise? In F. C. Blumberg & S. M. Fisch (Eds.), *Digital Games: A Context for Cognitive Development*. New Directions for Child and Adolescent Development, 139, 71–82.

8

Games for Learning: Vast Wasteland or a Digital Promise?

Michael H. Levine, Sarah E. Vaala

Abstract

*Research about emerging best practices in the learning sciences points to the
potential of deploying digital games as one possible solution to the twin challenges of weak student engagement and the need for more robust achievement
in literacy, science, technology, and math. This chapter reviews key cross-
cutting themes in this special volume, drawing perspective from the context of
the current United States program and policy reform. The authors conclude
that digital games have some unique potential to address pressing educational
challenges, but that new mechanisms for advancing purposeful research and
development must be adopted by both policymakers and industry leaders.
© 2013 Wiley Periodicals, Inc.*

NEW DIRECTIONS FOR CHILD AND ADOLESCENT DEVELOPMENT, no. 139, Spring 2013 © Wiley Periodicals, Inc.
Published online in Wiley Online Library (wileyonlinelibrary.com). • DOI: 10.1002/cad.20033

Take a look around the neighborhood. Whether you observe families at a restaurant, in a grocery store, or on a bus, you can't miss changes in adult–child interactions from just a generation ago. Everyone is plugged in, especially children. According to recent tracking studies from Common Sense Media, Sesame Workshop, and the Kaiser Family Foundation, the digital age is transforming children's media consumption and social interaction habits (Rideout, 2011; Rideout, Foehr, & Roberts, 2010; Gutnick, Robb, Takeuchi, & Kotler, 2011). Children as young as 4 years old have increasingly sophisticated digital lives, and 10-year-olds partake in more than 7 hours of media consumption a day— almost an hour and a quarter of which is used to play digital games!

These high consumption rates have inspired understandable concern in research and policy circles about how smartphones, iPads, and gaming devices may be compromising both childhood and parenting. Professionals and children's advocates are concerned that the panoply of media choices, many of which have limited educational value (Shuler, 2007) has become a new "vast wasteland." These observers cite former Federal Communications Chairman Newton Minow's famous summary of available television choices in the 1960s as an apt metaphor for current day offerings.

Five decades after Minow's speech, the marketplace of digital media choices, of course, is remarkably different. Perhaps we are at an exciting crossroads, because unlike the early days of television, where pioneers such as *Sesame Street* and *Mr. Rogers' Neighborhood* were few and far between, digital media and, in particular, games, have attracted investors, creators, and policymakers to explore their largely untapped potential (Richards, Stebbins, & Moellering, in press). The Entertainment Software Association (ESA, 2012) reports that 70% of households play on gaming consoles, while 38% report gameplay on their smartphone and 26% play digital games on other wireless devices (e.g., iPads). Notably, 59% of parents play digital games with their children. Of those parents, 90% think that games are "fun for the entire family," while 66% think games "provide mental stimulation" (ESA, 2012).

Today's digital games industry is perhaps still best known as a $55 billion worldwide video game entertainment behemoth that conjures images of mayhem and adolescent bonding (e.g., American Academy of Pediatrics [AAP], 2009; Ferguson, 2008; Kutner, Olson, Warner, & Hertzog, 2008). But as the articles in this timely volume illustrate, digital games have emerged as much more than that. Driven by their highly visual and engaging nature, games are now found everywhere, from medical and military simulations, to physical education courses, to publishing and advertising, and to corporate training.

This volume expertly draws on new research that shows how and why digital games may help advance an exciting new frontier of research on the changing ecology of human development (see Takeuchi, 2011; Takeuchi & Levine, in press). At the Joan Ganz Cooney Center at Sesame Workshop, our research and program activities have focused on digital games for a variety of reasons: First, they are an increasingly ubiquitous and engaging social exchange form across generations and income groups; second, there are a growing number of research-based models emerging as potential best practices to improve learning and healthy development outcomes; and third, they have potential to bridge the learning that children can do across life domains and settings (Thai, Lowenstein, Ching, & Rejeski, 2009).

In the past few years, a great deal of attention has been paid to the potential of digital games for good—President Barack Obama recently appointed an expert adviser to fashion the first national policy initiative on digital games' role in education, health, civic engagement, and numerous other areas (Toppo, 2012). The Department of Defense, National Science Foundation, and National Institutes of Health have all expanded research and development funding to tease out the range of effects that games, when well deployed, can play.

To fully engage and inspire children on subjects like math and science, educators and parents are beginning to take advantage of children's natural affinity for digital games. Games have attracted foundations' and policymakers' interest and may emerge as a new place to find common ground. For example, the Quest to Learn charter school in New York City, supported by the MacArthur Foundation and others, is the nation's first public school grounded in principles of game design. Chicago Quest, following the Quest to Learn model, opened in 2011. The premise behind these schools is simple: Allow young people, through gaming and game design, to construct their own learning environments. They will, in turn, develop the essential skills necessary to cooperate and problem solve in the 21st century economy.

There are several other significant examples of the new national interest in gaming as an emerging educational tool. In 2010, the Obama Administration launched a national effort to develop educational digital games—The National STEM (Science, Technology, Engineering and Math) Video Game Challenge—in cooperation with a wide range of philanthropic nonprofit children's organizations and industry partners. The effort seeks to overcome what the Gates Foundation has labeled a national "student engagement crisis" (Civic Enterprises, 2006) by encouraging youth to create their own game-based solutions to teach essential knowledge and skills. In 2011, Congress also launched a bipartisan E-Tech Caucus and supported a new Digital Promise initiative to promote public–private partnerships that advance innovation (including game-based solutions) in education (Levine, 2011).

This volume delves deeply into some of the critical issues that scholars, as well as program and policy experts, will need to examine in order to form a more critical analysis of the emerging game-infused educational interventions to advance learning and development. We turn now to some of the key themes and insights we draw from the issue.

NEW DIRECTIONS FOR CHILD AND ADOLESCENT DEVELOPMENT • DOI: 10.1002/cad

Cross-Cutting Issues

The articles in this volume of *New Directions for Child and Adolescent Development* take crucial steps in advancing the existing research base regarding youth and digital gameplay. Like so many other facets of kids and media research, the aspects we best understand about youth and digital games are those that are easiest to measure. We know that children and adolescents are spending a fair amount of time playing games in the home (Rideout, Foehr, & Roberts, 2010), at school (Millstone, 2012a; Public Broadcasting System [PBS], 2012), and, increasingly, while on-the-go using mobile devices (ESA, 2012; Lenhart, 2009; Rideout, Foehr, & Roberts, 2010). Recent estimates suggest that youth between ages 8–18 spend more than an hour a day playing digital games on average (i.e., 73 minutes; Rideout et al., 2010), a considerable increase over the average of 26 minutes per day in 1999 (Rideout, Foehr, Roberts, & Brodie, 1999).

We know too that amidst all the video game appeal from youth, parents often hold mixed perceptions of the role and repercussions of these media in their children's development. Many are concerned with the possible antisocial influences of violent games, as well as the time game play may displace from other activities (e.g., Gentile & Walsh, 2002; Kutner et al., 2008; Woodard & Gridina, 2000). Increasingly, however, parents feel that digital games can have a positive impact on children's learning (ESA, 2012). As the authors in this volume point out, our knowledge of the actual impact of digital games for children's health and development and the explanations for those effects are far less understood, though the research base is growing.

The articles here make strides in teasing out what the current body of literature can tell us about children's learning from digital game play and in illuminating important paths for developing our knowledge further. Each article examines closely a specific piece of the digital games and youth development puzzle. Specifically, rather than asking "do digital games have positive effects?" the authors consider more targeted questions regarding the nature of engagement and certain health and cognitive implications for youth. This is a particular strength of this volume, as investigating children's digital game use from multiple and defined angles is crucial to advancing the field and informing game development. Digital games are not monolithic; neither are young people or their circumstances, abilities, and needs. Accordingly, we should not expect that all games will impact all youth in the same way. It is our opinion that overly simplistic research questions and designs are in part to blame for the lack of clear or consistent findings in this area (see also Young et al., 2012). In fact, research methodology should match the multidimensionality of our youth and the digital games with which they engage.

Each article in this special journal issue contends that well-designed digital games can have positive influence on various, well-defined aspects

NEW DIRECTIONS FOR CHILD AND ADOLESCENT DEVELOPMENT • DOI: 10.1002/cad

interactive game, and face-to-face support and scaffolding in a teacher-led hands-on activity.

Still, one medium can reinforce the lessons conveyed by another only if they share the same (or closely related) educational content. Thus, for such benefits to arise, educational content must be closely aligned across media. Further, parallel to Fisch and Truglio's (2001) observation about *Sesame Street*, children must *recognize* this alignment to draw the connections necessary to gain the benefits of reinforcement across multiple media, as opposed to processing and learning from each experience in isolation.

Transfer of Learning as a Mechanism for Cross-Platform Learning

All three studies discussed earlier employed pre–post assessments whose tasks were different than those seen in the materials, although they reflected similar underlying educational content. Accordingly, the significant pretest–posttest effects in all three studies reflect *transfer of learning* (i.e., the learners' ability to apply concepts or skills acquired in one context to a new problem or context). Outside the realm of media, numerous theoretical mechanisms have been offered to explain how and when transfer of learning occurs in formal education and problem solving (e.g., Gentner, 1983; Greeno, Moore, & Smith, 1993; Holyoak, 1985; Salomon & Perkins, 1989; Schwartz, Bransford, & Sears, 2005). Elements of these approaches have been used to explain how transfer operates in informal education, such as educational television (Fisch, 2004).

However, data from the *Cyberchase* study also provided evidence of another form of transfer of learning—one that appears to lend insight into mechanisms at work in cross-platform learning. In this study, apart from the hands-on problem-solving assessments employed in the pretest and posttest, problem solving was also measured via online tracking data that recorded every mouse click while children played three *Cyberchase* online math games. Coding schemes used patterns of children's responses and errors to gain insight into the sophistication of the mathematical problem-solving strategies children used to play the games and the number of correct answers they produced. (See Fisch, Lesh, Motoki, Crespo, & Melfi, 2011, for a detailed discussion of this methodology.)

Online tracking data were compared between the treatment group that only used the games and the group that used multiple *Cyberchase* media components. Children who used multiple media employed significantly more sophisticated mathematical strategies while playing the three online games (e.g., additive vs. simple matching strategies), and produced more correct responses while playing two of the three games. As in the posttest tasks, children appeared to take the educational content they encountered in one medium (television and/or hands-on activities) and apply it while engaging with math content in another medium (online games). Such transfer of learning supported their interaction with the second medium, allowing children to apply more sophisticated approaches and producing a richer, more successful engagement with the material.

This, I believe, is a unique, key characteristic of cross-platform learning: The lessons learned from one medium can be applied, not only to enhance children's general knowledge (as manifest in posttest assessments), but also to support and enrich children's experience *while they are in the process of learning from a second medium*. This richer engagement, coupled with the factors discussed earlier regarding multiple entry points and varied practice, results in the stronger pretest–posttest effects observed for cross-platform learning as compared to learning from a single medium.

Indeed, it is quite possible that cross-platform learning may not only provide opportunities for transfer of learning, but that the presence of the same characters and contexts across media may even facilitate such transfer. Research on transfer of learning has shown that it is more likely to occur when two situations appear similar on their face (*surface structure similarity*) than when they are dissimilar on their surface but rest on similar underlying principles (*deep structure similarity*; e.g., Bassok & Holyoak, 1993; Gentner & Forbus, 1991). Thus, encountering *Cyberchase* characters in an online game might lead children to think of other times when they saw the same characters (e.g., on television). This could facilitate the transfer of information and skills from one medium to another in a way that seeing different characters on television and in a game might not.

This hypothesis is supported by data from the *Between the Lions* study, in which children viewed *Between the Lions* videos either in isolation or with hands-on materials that either featured or did not feature illustrations of *Between the Lions* characters. The resulting effects did not attain statistical significance, but nonsignificant trends were found in the expected direction: Use of the videos plus hands-on materials with *Between the Lions* characters produced stronger gains in literacy than use of the videos alone. However, use of equivalent hands-on materials without *Between the Lions* characters did not produce such effects. (In fact, the impact of videos plus generic hands-on materials was actually smaller than that of videos alone.) As Fisch and Truglio (2001) would predict, the alignment between the educational content of the videos and hands-on materials was insufficient to produce greater learning by itself; rather, children had to recognize the connection between the two, and the presence of shared characters helped children make those connections.

Limitations of Cross-Platform Learning

If transfer across media is indeed a key mechanism at work in cross-platform learning, then factors that facilitate or inhibit transfer of learning

NEW DIRECTIONS FOR CHILD AND ADOLESCENT DEVELOPMENT • DOI: 10.1002/cad

should operate similarly in facilitating or inhibiting cross-platform learning. It is worth noting that, even in formal education or controlled experimental settings, transfer of learning often does not occur (e.g., Detterman, 1993). To achieve successful transfer, learners must comprehend the initial presentation of content, create a mental representation of the content that is sufficiently abstract to extend beyond the context in which the content was initially encountered, and recognize the content as relevant to the new situation in which it might be applied. A failure at any of these stages—such as a lack of initial comprehension, a mental representation that is too narrow or context-bound, or a failure to recognize a potential application—would result in a failure to find transfer of learning (Bransford, Brown, & Cocking, 1999; Fisch, 2004).

With that in mind, let us return to the point that all three studies reviewed above found that pretest–posttest effects were not always strongest in the group that used the greatest number of media components, and consider the explanations that the researchers posited for these trends. Fisch and colleagues (2010) suggested that *Panwapa*'s impact on particular aspects of global citizenship appeared most clearly in whichever treatment groups used the components that addressed those aspects most strongly. For example, use of the website was associated with effects on children's ability to identify their own and other countries, probably because country names were integral to children's login names and navigation. Piotrowski and her colleagues (in press) hypothesized that the patterns of differences observed for *Between the Lions* could be attributed to the complexity of the various literacy skills they assessed and the age and prior ability of the participating children. For more basic skills, benefits of cross-platform learning appeared for kindergartners but not younger children, perhaps because kindergartners were able to make the necessary connections between the televised and hands-on materials. By contrast, younger children's limited cognitive capacity was overtaxed by the greater assortment of televised and hands-on materials, preventing them from experiencing the benefits of cross-platform learning. Fisch and colleagues (in press) also pointed to the amount of *Cyberchase* material used in their study to explain why effects were often stronger for users of videos and online games than for users of these media plus hands-on activities. Instead of addressing the amount of material from the standpoint of children's cognitive capacity, however, they raised the issue from the perspective of teachers who were faced with the challenge of making time for the materials in their busy school day. Since this challenge was greatest for teachers whose classes used all of the materials, Fisch and colleagues suggested that these classes may not have used the materials as thoroughly, or that children in this treatment group may have picked up on cues to their teachers' dissatisfaction.

It is difficult to know which of these possible explanations may be correct, or whether all of these factors actually may play a role. Nevertheless,

NEW DIRECTIONS FOR CHILD AND ADOLESCENT DEVELOPMENT • DOI: 10.1002/cad

the latter two explanations highlight a key issue for multiple-media approaches to education: How much media is too much? Is there an optimal level of educational media use, beyond which—given children's cognitive capacity and/or the needs, constraints, and attitudes of adult gatekeepers—the benefits of cross-platform learning are diminished? Further research will be needed to identify optimal approaches, with important implications for the design of educationally effective materials for cross-platform learning.

Another essential, but unanswered, question concerns developmental differences in cross-platform learning. Some nonmedia studies of transfer of learning, in areas such as analogical reasoning and metaphor, have found the likelihood of transfer to increase with age (e.g., Brown, Kane, & Long, 1989; Gentner, 1988), perhaps because older children can draw on a greater knowledge base or because they are better able to appreciate underlying relational structure instead of relying merely on surface features. To the degree that the benefits of cross-platform learning stem from transfer, it is reasonable to expect that older children may be better able to transfer content and skills across media, and thus benefit more from cross-platform learning. Indeed, Piotrowski and colleagues (in press) found greater effects of multiple media among 6-year-olds than 4-year-olds, although Fisch and colleagues (2010) found main effects of age (4 to 7 years) but no significant interactions between age and the impact of different combinations of *Panwapa* materials. (Data from Fisch and colleagues' in press study of *Cyberchase* do not directly address developmental issues, because all the participating children were approximately the same age.) It seems likely that different patterns of developmental differences might arise, depending on factors such as the nature of the educational content being addressed or the number and types of media components used. However, existing studies have only begun to address this issue, so further research is needed to gain a greater understanding of ways in which development interacts with characteristics of both materials and users to impact on learning.

Conclusion

Since cross-platform learning is a newly emerging field, it is not surprising that many key questions have yet to be answered. That said, the studies conducted to date have already taken the essential first step of demonstrating the potential of cross-platform approaches to promote learning outcomes beyond those of a single medium. Moreover, transfer of learning appears to provide a promising direction in explaining the mechanisms that underlie the effects of cross-platform learning, as children apply knowledge and skills gained from one medium to produce richer engagement while in the process of learning from a second medium. As the media landscape continues to move further in the direction of projects that employ multiple media platforms, future research will be invaluable both in helping us understand children's interactions with these media and in identifying ways in which such crossmedia approaches can be used most effectively for education.

References

Bassok, M., & Holyoak, K. J. (1993). Pragmatic knowledge and conceptual structure: Determinants of transfer across quantitative domains. In D. K. Detterman & R. J. Sternberg (Eds.), *Transfer on trial: Intelligence, cognition, and instruction* (pp. 68–98). Norwood, NJ: Ablex.

Bransford, J. D., Brown, A. L., & Cocking, R. R. (Eds.). (1999). *How people learn: Brain, mind, experience, and school*. Washington, DC: National Academy Press.

Brown, A. L., Kane, M. I., & Long, C. (1989). Analogical transfer in young children: Analogies as tools for communication and exposition. *Applied Cognitive Psychology, 3*, 275–293.

Detterman, D. K. (1993). The case for the prosecution: Transfer as an epiphenomenon. In D. K. Detterman & R. J. Sternberg (Eds.), *Transfer on trial: Intelligence, cognition, and instruction* (pp. 1–24). Norwood, NJ: Ablex.

Dunn, K., & Dunn, R. (1987). Disputing outmoded beliefs about student learning. *Educational Leadership, 44*(6), 55–62.

Dunn, R., Griggs, S. A., Olson, J., Beasley, M., & Gorman, B. S. (1995). A meta-analytic validation of the Dunn and Dunn model of learning-style preferences. *Journal of Educational Research, 88*, 353–362.

Fisch, S. M. (2004). *Children's learning from educational television: Sesame Street and beyond*. Mahwah, NJ: Lawrence Erlbaum.

Fisch, S. M. (2009). Educational television and interactive media for children: Effects on academic knowledge, skills, and attitudes. In J. Bryant & M. B. Oliver (Eds.), *Media effects: Advances in theory and research* (3rd ed.; pp. 402–435). New York, NY: Routledge.

Fisch, S. M., Hsueh, Y., Zhou, Z., Xu, C. J., Hamed, M., Khader, Z., . . . Guha, M. L. (2010). Crossing borders: Learning from educational media in four countries. *Televizion, 23*(1), 42–45.

Fisch, S. M., Lesh, R., Motoki, E., Crespo, S., & Melfi, V. (2011). Children's mathematical reasoning in online games: Can data mining reveal strategic thinking? *Child Development Perspectives, 5*, 88–92.

Fisch, S. M., Lesh, R., Motoki, E., Crespo, S., & Melfi, V. (in press). Cross-platform learning: How do children learn from multiple media? In F. C. Blumberg (Ed.), *Learning by playing: Frontiers of video gaming in education*. New York, NY: Oxford University Press.

Fisch, S. M., & Truglio, R. T. (2001). Why children learn from *Sesame Street*. In S. M. Fisch & R. T. Truglio (Eds.), *"G" is for growing: Thirty years of research on children and Sesame Street* (pp. 233–244). Mahwah, NJ: Lawrence Erlbaum Associates.

Gentner, D. (1983). Structure-mapping: A theoretical framework for analogy. *Cognitive Science, 7*, 155–170.

Gentner, D. (1988). Metaphor as structure mapping: The relational shift. *Child Development, 59*, 47–59.

Gentner, D., & Forbus, K. D. (1991). MAC/FAC: A model of similarity-based retrieval. *Cognitive Science, 19*, 141–205.

Gick, M. L., & Holyoak, K. J. (1983). Schema induction and analogical transfer. *Cognitive Psychology, 15*, 1–38.

Greeno, J. G., Moore, J. L., & Smith, D. R. (1993). Transfer of situated knowledge. In D. K. Detterman & R. J. Sternberg (Eds.), *Transfer on trial: Intelligence, cognition, and instruction* (pp. 99–167). Norwood, NJ: Ablex.

Holyoak, K. J. (1985). The pragmatics of analogical transfer. In G. H. Bower (Ed.), *The psychology of learning and motivation* (pp. 59–87). New York, NY: Academic Press.

Honey, M. A., & Hilton, M. L. (2012). *Learning science through computer games and simulations.* Washington, DC: National Academies Press.

Kirkorian, H. L., & Anderson, D. R. (2011). Learning from educational media. In S. L. Calvert & B. J. Wilson (Eds.), *The handbook of children, media, and development* (pp. 188–213). West Sussex, England: Wiley-Blackwell.

Linebarger, D. L., Kosanic, A. Z., Greenwood, C. R., & Doku, N. S. (2004). Effects of viewing the television program *Between the Lions* on the emergent literacy skills of young children. *Journal of Educational Psychology, 96*(2), 297–308.

Linebarger, D. L., & McMenamin, K. (2010). *Evaluation of the* Between the Lions *Mississippi literacy initiative, 2008–2009.* Philadelphia, PA: Annenberg School for Communication, University of Pennsylvania.

Norman, D. A. (1988). *The design of everyday things.* New York, NY: Basic Books.

Piotrowski, J. T., Jennings, N., & Linebarger, D. L. (in press). Extending the lessons of educational television with young American children. *Journal of Children and Media.*

Rabinowitz, M., Blumberg, F. C., & Everson, H. T. (Eds.). (2004). *The design of instruction and evaluation: Affordances of using media and technology.* Mahwah, NJ: Lawrence Erlbaum Associates.

Salomon, G., & Perkins, D. N. (1989). Rocky roads to transfer: Rethinking mechanisms of a neglected phenomenon. *Educational Psychologist, 24*(2), 113–142.

Schwartz, D. L., Bransford, J. D., & Sears, D. L. (2005). Efficiency and innovation in transfer. In J. Mestre (Ed.), *Transfer of learning from a modern multidisciplinary perspective* (pp. 1–51). Greenwich, CT: Information Age Publishing.

Singley, M. K., & Anderson, J. R. (1989). *The transfer of cognitive skill.* Cambridge, MA: Harvard University Press.

SHALOM M. FISCH is president and founder of MediaKidz Research & Consulting, New Jersey, USA, and can be reached via e-mail at mediakidz@lycos.com.

NEW DIRECTIONS FOR CHILD AND ADOLESCENT DEVELOPMENT • DOI: 10.1002/cad

Levine, M. H., & Vaala, S. E. (2013). Games for learning: Vast wasteland or a digital promise? In F. C. Blumberg & S. M. Fisch (Eds.), *Digital Games: A Context for Cognitive Development*. New Directions for Child and Adolescent Development, 139, 71–82.

8

Games for Learning: Vast Wasteland or a Digital Promise?

Michael H. Levine, Sarah E. Vaala

Abstract

Research about emerging best practices in the learning sciences points to the potential of deploying digital games as one possible solution to the twin challenges of weak student engagement and the need for more robust achievement in literacy, science, technology, and math. This chapter reviews key crosscutting themes in this special volume, drawing perspective from the context of the current United States program and policy reform. The authors conclude that digital games have some unique potential to address pressing educational challenges, but that new mechanisms for advancing purposeful research and development must be adopted by both policymakers and industry leaders. © 2013 Wiley Periodicals, Inc.

Take a look around the neighborhood. Whether you observe families at a restaurant, in a grocery store, or on a bus, you can't miss changes in adult–child interactions from just a generation ago. Everyone is plugged in, especially children. According to recent tracking studies from Common Sense Media, Sesame Workshop, and the Kaiser Family Foundation, the digital age is transforming children's media consumption and social interaction habits (Rideout, 2011; Rideout, Foehr, & Roberts, 2010; Gutnick, Robb, Takeuchi, & Kotler, 2011). Children as young as 4 years old have increasingly sophisticated digital lives, and 10-year-olds partake in more than 7 hours of media consumption a day— almost an hour and a quarter of which is used to play digital games!

These high consumption rates have inspired understandable concern in research and policy circles about how smartphones, iPads, and gaming devices may be compromising both childhood and parenting. Professionals and children's advocates are concerned that the panoply of media choices, many of which have limited educational value (Shuler, 2007) has become a new "vast wasteland." These observers cite former Federal Communications Chairman Newton Minow's famous summary of available television choices in the 1960s as an apt metaphor for current day offerings.

Five decades after Minow's speech, the marketplace of digital media choices, of course, is remarkably different. Perhaps we are at an exciting crossroads, because unlike the early days of television, where pioneers such as *Sesame Street* and *Mr. Rogers' Neighborhood* were few and far between, digital media and, in particular, games, have attracted investors, creators, and policymakers to explore their largely untapped potential (Richards, Stebbins, & Moellering, in press). The Entertainment Software Association (ESA, 2012) reports that 70% of households play on gaming consoles, while 38% report gameplay on their smartphone and 26% play digital games on other wireless devices (e.g., iPads). Notably, 59% of parents play digital games with their children. Of those parents, 90% think that games are "fun for the entire family," while 66% think games "provide mental stimulation" (ESA, 2012).

Today's digital games industry is perhaps still best known as a $55 billion worldwide video game entertainment behemoth that conjures images of mayhem and adolescent bonding (e.g., American Academy of Pediatrics [AAP], 2009; Ferguson, 2008; Kutner, Olson, Warner, & Hertzog, 2008). But as the articles in this timely volume illustrate, digital games have emerged as much more than that. Driven by their highly visual and engaging nature, games are now found everywhere, from medical and military simulations, to physical education courses, to publishing and advertising, and to corporate training.

This volume expertly draws on new research that shows how and why digital games may help advance an exciting new frontier of research on the changing ecology of human development (see Takeuchi, 2011; Takeuchi & Levine, in press). At the Joan Ganz Cooney Center at Sesame Workshop, our research and program activities have focused on digital games for a variety of reasons: First, they are an increasingly ubiquitous and engaging social exchange form across generations and income groups; second, there are a growing number of research-based models emerging as potential best practices to improve learning and healthy development outcomes; and third, they have potential to bridge the learning that children can do across life domains and settings (Thai, Lowenstein, Ching, & Rejeski, 2009).

In the past few years, a great deal of attention has been paid to the potential of digital games for good—President Barack Obama recently appointed an expert adviser to fashion the first national policy initiative on digital games' role in education, health, civic engagement, and numerous other areas (Toppo, 2012). The Department of Defense, National Science Foundation, and National Institutes of Health have all expanded research and development funding to tease out the range of effects that games, when well deployed, can play.

To fully engage and inspire children on subjects like math and science, educators and parents are beginning to take advantage of children's natural affinity for digital games. Games have attracted foundations' and policymakers' interest and may emerge as a new place to find common ground. For example, the Quest to Learn charter school in New York City, supported by the MacArthur Foundation and others, is the nation's first public school grounded in principles of game design. Chicago Quest, following the Quest to Learn model, opened in 2011. The premise behind these schools is simple: Allow young people, through gaming and game design, to construct their own learning environments. They will, in turn, develop the essential skills necessary to cooperate and problem solve in the 21st century economy.

There are several other significant examples of the new national interest in gaming as an emerging educational tool. In 2010, the Obama Administration launched a national effort to develop educational digital games—The National STEM (Science, Technology, Engineering and Math) Video Game Challenge—in cooperation with a wide range of philanthropic nonprofit children's organizations and industry partners. The effort seeks to overcome what the Gates Foundation has labeled a national "student engagement crisis" (Civic Enterprises, 2006) by encouraging youth to create their own game-based solutions to teach essential knowledge and skills. In 2011, Congress also launched a bipartisan E-Tech Caucus and supported a new Digital Promise initiative to promote public–private partnerships that advance innovation (including game-based solutions) in education (Levine, 2011).

This volume delves deeply into some of the critical issues that scholars, as well as program and policy experts, will need to examine in order to form a more critical analysis of the emerging game-infused educational interventions to advance learning and development. We turn now to some of the key themes and insights we draw from the issue.

New Directions for Child and Adolescent Development • DOI: 10.1002/cad

Cross-Cutting Issues

The articles in this volume of *New Directions for Child and Adolescent Development* take crucial steps in advancing the existing research base regarding youth and digital gameplay. Like so many other facets of kids and media research, the aspects we best understand about youth and digital games are those that are easiest to measure. We know that children and adolescents are spending a fair amount of time playing games in the home (Rideout, Foehr, & Roberts, 2010), at school (Millstone, 2012a; Public Broadcasting System [PBS], 2012), and, increasingly, while on-the-go using mobile devices (ESA, 2012; Lenhart, 2009; Rideout, Foehr, & Roberts, 2010). Recent estimates suggest that youth between ages 8–18 spend more than an hour a day playing digital games on average (i.e., 73 minutes; Rideout et al., 2010), a considerable increase over the average of 26 minutes per day in 1999 (Rideout, Foehr, Roberts, & Brodie, 1999).

We know too that amidst all the video game appeal from youth, parents often hold mixed perceptions of the role and repercussions of these media in their children's development. Many are concerned with the possible antisocial influences of violent games, as well as the time game play may displace from other activities (e.g., Gentile & Walsh, 2002; Kutner et al., 2008; Woodard & Gridina, 2000). Increasingly, however, parents feel that digital games can have a positive impact on children's learning (ESA, 2012). As the authors in this volume point out, our knowledge of the actual impact of digital games for children's health and development and the explanations for those effects are far less understood, though the research base is growing.

The articles here make strides in teasing out what the current body of literature can tell us about children's learning from digital game play and in illuminating important paths for developing our knowledge further. Each article examines closely a specific piece of the digital games and youth development puzzle. Specifically, rather than asking "do digital games have positive effects?" the authors consider more targeted questions regarding the nature of engagement and certain health and cognitive implications for youth. This is a particular strength of this volume, as investigating children's digital game use from multiple and defined angles is crucial to advancing the field and informing game development. Digital games are not monolithic; neither are young people or their circumstances, abilities, and needs. Accordingly, we should not expect that all games will impact all youth in the same way. It is our opinion that overly simplistic research questions and designs are in part to blame for the lack of clear or consistent findings in this area (see also Young et al., 2012). In fact, research methodology should match the multidimensionality of our youth and the digital games with which they engage.

Each article in this special journal issue contends that well-designed digital games can have positive influence on various, well-defined aspects of children's and adolescents' health and learning. The authors also go a step further by considering potential *mechanisms* operating between youth's digital gaming and their health and development. This approach is welcome, as understanding the forces at work between inputs (e.g., exposure to digital games) and outputs (e.g., learning; healthy behavior) is key to identifying the features that are successful or unsuccessful for accomplishing certain learning goals. Explicating potential mechanisms introduces to the field testable predictions of what is happening in the "black box" that exists between digital game play and youth outcomes. Testing those predictions will then result in tangible, research-driven insights for best practices in designing digital games that will be most advantageous for youth.

A theme that weaves across several of the articles here is the role of children's *engagement* with digital games in determining the extent and nature of outcomes. For example, in his consideration of children's cross-platform participation with media properties, Fisch (this volume) highlights that access to multiple media—including digital games—offer youth numerous points of entry to educational content. With several options for media participation, it becomes more likely that children will find and use the medium or media that most appeal to their interests and learning styles and thus will be more likely to deeply engage with educational material through one or more platforms. Further expounding the concept of engagement, Sherry (this volume) marries Uses & Gratifications theory with developmental theory to explore how children's evolving game play motivations influence their engagement with various genres and features of games and, thus, the educational value they glean from digital game play. Deater-Deckard, Chang, and Evans (this volume) describe a model they have under development to define and measure three crucial sub-components of engagement—cognitive, affective, and behavioral—to determine how students' engagement may vary between traditional curricula and educational digital games and to inform appropriate educational game design.

In light of the important role engagement plays between digital game exposure and impact, several authors point to the need to design high-quality educational games that will appeal to youth as much as entertainment games do (i.e., Blumberg et al., Deater-Decker et al., Sherry, this volume). Since today's youth are "digital natives" whose lives have been immersed in technologies since birth, they are incredibly tech-savvy even at young ages (Prensky, 2001). They can tell instantly when a game has high-quality graphics, strong narratives, and the other hallmarks of popular commercially available entertainment games. Blumberg and colleagues stress that "[educational] game development efforts often fail to adequately consider the cognitive sophistication or relative immaturity of its child and adolescent audience, and the appeal of the games compared to more recreational ones" (this volume, p. 43). Attention to game appeal is crucial, since we can make highly educational digital games that teach everything from algebra to art to astronomy. However, if they fail to attract and engage youth, our efforts will be unfounded.

Securing the attention and support of parents and teachers is also crucial. In a 2007 parent survey conducted by the Joan Ganz Cooney Center, Common Sense Media, and Insight Research Group, we found that while parents of 6- to 14-year-olds believed that digital media broadly had great potential for children's learning, relatively few felt digital games boosted kids' curiosity and interest in learning (30%), math and science skills (28%), or reading and writing skills (19%). Clearly, more should be done to develop high-quality educational games and to get them into the consciousness and then the hands of the parents, teachers, and youth.

The article by Calvert, Staiano, and Bond (this volume) also reminds us that children do not play digital games in a vacuum. Rather, the social contexts of that play can have important repercussions for the nature and impact of their gaming. Further, these authors describe how careful consideration of content and context can make digital games—typically implicated as a contributor to rising obesity rates—into a promotional agent of healthful eating behaviors among children and adolescents.

Blumberg and colleagues (this volume) highlight the invaluable knowledge we gain by taking our inquiries to the experts themselves—the child and adolescent players. By asking children and adolescents to describe what they like most about digital game play, researchers have learned that children enjoy the opportunities to gain mastery, make their own choices and set difficulty levels, and use trial and error strategies in a setting where failure will not be graded or judged—all while being entertained.

Similarly, Revelle (this volume) describes the importance of user-centered approaches to digital game design; that is, beginning the design process from the perspective of the needs and abilities of the children or adolescents for whom the game is intended. Her article considers the interactions between children's cognitive and motor abilities and the interfaces and features that digital games may employ, stressing ultimately that the right match between game design and children's needs and capabilities drives "games' usability, appeal, and effectiveness" among players (p. 37). Together, the six articles in this volume indicate—explicitly or implicitly—that our focus should not be solely on digital games themselves, but also must incorporate the factors of the players (e.g., developmental stage; interests) and the physical and social contexts of their play.

Although it is not addressed here, children's co-play of digital games with parents and other caregivers is also an important avenue to consider through additional research. There has been a long history of focus on the benefits of parent–child "co-viewing" of television for boosting learning and mitigating potential harmful effects; we believe that co-engagement with digital games may have similar salutary impact for families (see

Chiong, 2009; Takeuchi & Stevens, 2011). When digital games are designed such that each party is engaged in play, parents can scaffold the educational content for their children and extend the learning outside the context of play. In addition, many parents report that they learn technological skills from their digital native children (Takeuchi, 2011). Using intergenerational digital game play as a method for promoting learning and parent–child bonding seems particularly appealing and feasible given the proportion of adults who report regular game play themselves.

One prominent example of development in this domain is underway at the Institute for Simulation & Training under the direction of Lori Walters. Walters and her group are developing a digital app to foster intergenerational learning. Specifically, Augmented Reality for Intergenerational Exploration (ARIGE) is a free smartphone app that applies a virtual layer to exploring the outdoors via geocaching, while fostering intergenerational communication and learning. Armed with a GPS/compass/camera-enabled smartphone, intergenerational teams comprised of youths and grandparents embark on a quest to gather virtual artifacts throughout Flushing Meadows Park, near the site of the 1964 World's Fair, and solve topical puzzles. The experience is designed to highlight the generational skills/knowledge of each member of the team. This effort and other intergenerational game opportunities await further investigation to illuminate best practices for designing educational games for play among children and their parents, or even grandparents.

Finally, while this volume addresses children's and adolescents' use of digital media produced *for* them, it is important to also recognize the powerful learning that can result when children design and program their own games. Kevin Clark and his colleagues at George Mason University have built a research program in which underserved youth are taught to design and create their own digital games at afterschool programs and with the help of mentors (see Clark, Brandt, Hopkins, & Wilhelm, 2010; Clark & Sheridan, 2010). These scholars and others have found that learning to design and program digital games helps youth to learn not only game programming skills, but also math, problem solving, critical thinking, systems thinking, and metacognitive skills (Clark et al., 2010; Torres, 2009). The process is empowering and also may build self-esteem. Again, further research is needed to explicate the full nature and extent of learning that may accompany game design and programming training, as well as methods for efficiently incorporating such curricula into formal education.

We believe the work reflected in the current volume moves the needle on our current understanding of the healthy development of youth in an increasingly digital world, and in particular the positive roles that well-designed digital games can play in their lives. But we hope this is only the beginning. Building from the foundations these authors have laid will help elucidate the many possible ways digital games can enrich children's and adolescents' education and well-being. In the following section, we

New Directions for Child and Adolescent Development • DOI: 10.1002/cad

suggest some next steps that our nation can take to clarify the mechanisms for those benefits, and to find best practices in digital game design.

Next Steps: Building the Potential of Digital Games for Change

At a White House event in 2011, U.S. Secretary of Education Arne Duncan announced the establishment of the Digital Promise, a nonprofit initiative created to promote digital technologies with the potential to transform teaching and learning. Experts on digital media and learning cheered this latest signal that robust experimentation with technology based on rigorous research and development would take a more prominent place in the national education reform debate. This section addresses some of the key challenges the field faces, which more research and development work on well-designed game-based-learning platforms might help address in the decade ahead.

The Literacy Crisis. Foundational literacy skills are completely stagnant among low-income and minority students; despite billions of dollars spent on early intervention in literacy, we have made scant progress in 25 years. Tragically, only one in six African American or Hispanic 4th graders is proficient in reading, according to the 2011 National Assessment of Educational Progress; time has run out on our 20th-century approach to this wholly preventable national disgrace. New evidence from the U.S. Department of Education's *Ready to Learn* programs shows significant gains in vocabulary-development and reading-comprehension skills that can be facilitated by embedded media, such as games that personalize and deepen literacy learning (e.g., Penuel et al., 2009). We need to know much more about how engaging literacy games can be delivered in multiple digital formats anytime, anywhere to promote learning "right from the start."

The Engagement Crisis. As Deater-Deckard and colleagues point out, "engagement drives moment-by-moment use, as well as the learning that occurs during play and preferably transfers afterwards" (p. 22). This is not what is happening within formal education among many youth, who are high media consumers but are dropping out of school in droves. According to Child Trends (2012), nearly one in five minority youths is dropping out of school, and in some lower socioeconomic communities, this number approached 50% in 2007 (Swanson, 2010). Clearly, school is neither engaging nor relevant to far too much of our youth. Can we square these data constructively with better designed, game-infused curricula, such as those being offered by pioneers like Quest to Learn?

The STEM and College Graduation Crises. According to recent international comparison data, U.S. students are falling further behind other industrialized countries in everything from math (25th place) and science scores (17th) to the proportion of young people with college degrees (14th; see Hechinger, 2010; U.S. Department of Education, 2012).

NEW DIRECTIONS FOR CHILD AND ADOLESCENT DEVELOPMENT • DOI: 10.1002/cad

The challenges our young people now face in an interconnected, digitally driven global landscape require a new set of competitive and cooperative skills. Design competitions and more active uses of project- or inquiry-based learning are gaining currency in high-performing schools. Can games be more integrated in these models as they are interactive and participatory?

Cooperative Learning. Games are increasingly social. Whether they involve teams jointly accomplishing missions, asynchronous collaboration over social networks, or sourcing advice from interest-driven communities to help solve tricky challenges, games may naturally drive peer-to-peer and peer-to-mentor social interactions. We need to test whether such social interaction can be a boon for learning or simply a "time dump" for bored and disengaged youth.

Development of 21st-Century Skills. Good games are complex. Whether it is a 5-year-old parsing a Pokémon card or a 15-year-old building in SimCity™, games can foster critical skills such as problem solving, critical thinking, creativity, collaboration, and systems thinking (Gee, 2007). Given that many of the jobs that will emerge in the 21st century have not yet been invented, these skills are particularly important. Will the current push to deeper, "common core" standards be aligned with the unique affordances of digital games to personalize and assess skills, knowledge, and perspectives?

Although many good models are beginning to be scaled up, a significant gap exists between the promise of game-based learning and the current reality. This gap is especially evident in transforming games from effective research trials into financially sustainable products that can reach and affect students through either formal or informal channels. To help close this gap, the Joan Ganz Cooney Center has recently undertaken a major project with the support of the Bill & Melinda Gates Foundation and the John L. and James S. Knight Foundation. The Games and Learning Publishing Council has conducted a business-market analysis, (Richards et al., in press), case studies of effective models (Millstone, 2012b), and a national survey of teachers to understand market dynamics, practitioner perspectives, and areas of innovation that are ready for scaling up (Millstone, 2012a). The council is releasing, on an ongoing basis, other market and policy analyses, along with research-based resources such as new games and a learning website for researchers, entrepreneurs, practitioners, and funders.

To increase the capacity of researchers and industry to address the issues raised here, we join others in calling for more robust investments in research. Most R&D is provided by the government—the Department of Defense, the Department of Education, National Science Foundation (NSF), and the National Institutes of Health (NIH) all support game-based experimental research. However, it is unevenly distributed, highly fragmented, and lacks shared research priorities or mechanisms to foster interagency coordination and collaboration. The Federal Games Working Group led by the White House Office on Science and Technology Policy has made progress in establishing a mechanism for interagency collaboration, planning, and data sharing that should help guide future programs for research and development. As research advances, we need to know more precisely what is being done in the field: government should regularly publish inventories that track what research is being funded and by which agencies.

As this volume makes clear, the learning potential of digital games has yet to be fully realized. Much work remains to use their distinctive qualities to personalize learning while aligning with educational standards, and promoting good health. As the technology industry disrupts old practice models, policymakers and industry leaders may well look to the power of digital games to help build a modern education system. Only then will every child have a fair shot to realize their promise.

References

American Academy of Pediatrics. (2009). Policy statement—Media violence. *Pediatrics, 124*(5), 1495–1503.

Child Trends. (2012). *High school dropout rates: Indicators on children and youth.* Retrieved from www.childtrendsdatabank.org/sites/default/files/01_Dropout_Rates.pdf

Chiong, C. (2009). *Can video games promote intergenerational play & literacy learning? Report from a research and design workshop.* New York, NY: Joan Ganz Cooney Center at Sesame Workshop. Retrieved from http://joanganzcooneycenter.org/upload_kits/intergen_final_021210.pdf

Civic Enterprises in association with Peter D. Hart Research Associates. (2006, March). *The silent epidemic: Perspectives of high school dropouts.* Seattle, WA: The Bill & Melinda Gates Foundation. Retrieved from www.gatesfoundation.org/united-states/Documents/TheSilentEpidemic3-06FINAL.pdf

Clark, K., Brandt, J., Hopkins, R., & Wilhelm, J. (2010). Making games after school: Participatory game design in non-formal learning environments. *Educational Technology, 49*(6), 40–44.

Clark, K., & Sheridan, K. (2010). Game design through mentoring and collaboration. *Journal of Educational Multimedia and Hypermedia, 19*(2), 5–22.

Entertainment Software Association. (2012). *2012 Sales, demographic and usage data: Essential facts about the computer and video game industry.* Retrieved from www.theesa.com/facts/pdfs/ESA_EF_2012.pdf

Ferguson, C. J. (2008). The school shooting/violent video game link: Causal relationship or moral panic? *Journal of Investigative Psychology and Offender Profiling, 5,* 25–37.

Gee, J. P. (2007). *What video games have to teach us about learning and literacy* (2nd ed.). New York, NY: Macmillan.

Gentile, D. A., & Walsh, D. A. (2002). A normative study of family media habits. *Applied Developmental Psychology, 23,* 157–178.

Gutnick, A. L., Robb, M., Takeuchi, L., & Kotler, J. (2011). *Always connected: The new digital media habits of young children.* New York, NY: Joan Ganz Cooney Center at Sesame Workshop. Retrieved from www.joanganzcooneycenter.org/publication/always-connected-the-new-digital-media-habits-of-young-children/

Hechinger, J. (2010, December 7). U.S. teens lag as China soars on international test. *Bloomberg.com*. Retrieved from www.bloomberg.com/news/2010-12-07/teens-in-u-s -rank-25th-on-math-test-trail-in-science-reading.html

Kutner, L. A., Olson, C. K., Warner, D. E., & Hertzog, S. M. (2008). Parents' and sons' perspectives on video game play: A qualitative study. *Journal of Adolescent Research, 23*(1), 76–96.

Lenhart, A. (2009). *Teens and mobile phones over the past five years: Pew Internet looks back*. Menlo Park, CA: Kaiser Family Foundation.

Levine, M. H. (2011, March 11). *Congress launches caucus for competitiveness in entertainment technology*. [Blog post]. Retrieved from www.joanganzcooneycenter.org /Cooney-Center-Blog-127.html

Millstone, J. (2012a). *Teacher attitudes about digital games in the classroom*. New York, NY: Joan Ganz Cooney Center at Sesame Workshop in collaboration with Brain-POP®. Retrieved from www.joanganzcooneycenter.org/images/presentation/jgcc _teacher_survey.pdf

Millstone, J. (2012b). *National survey and video case studies: Teacher attitudes about digital games in the class room*. New York, NY: Joan Ganz Cooney Center at Sesame Workshop in collaboration with BrainPOP®. Retrieved from http://joanganzcooney center.org/Reports-34.html

Penuel, W. R., Pasnik, S., Bates, L., Townsend, E., Gallagher, L. P., Llorente, C., & Hupert, N. (2009). *Preschool teachers can use a media-rich curriculum to prepare low-income children for school success: Results of a randomized controlled trial*. New York, NY, and Menlo Park, CA: Education Development Center, Inc., and SRI International.

Prensky, M. (2001). Digital natives, digital immigrants. *On the Horizon, 9*, 1–6.

Public Broadcasting System. (2012). *National PBS survey finds teachers want more access to classroom tech*. Retrieved from www.pbs.org/about/news/archive/2012 /teacher-survey-fetc/

Richards, J., Stebbins, L., & Moellering, K. (in press). *Games for a digital age: K–12 market map and investment analysis*. New York, NY: Joan Ganz Cooney Center at Sesame Workshop.

Rideout, V. J. (2011). *Zero to eight: Children's media use in America*. San Francisco, CA: Common Sense Media.

Rideout, V. J., Foehr, U. G., & Roberts, D. F. (2010). *Generation M²: Media in the lives of 8- to 18-year-olds*. Menlo Park, CA: Kaiser Family Foundation.

Rideout, V. J., Foehr, U. G., Roberts, D. F., & Brodie, M. (1999). *Kids & media @ the new millennium*. Menlo Park, CA: Kaiser Family Foundation.

Shuler, C. (2007). *D is for digital. An analysis of the children's interactive media environment with a focus on mass marketed products that promote learning*. New York, NY: Joan Ganz Cooney Center at Sesame Workshop. Retrieved from http://joangan-zcooneycenter.org/upload_kits/disfordigital_reports.pdf

Swanson, C. B. (2010, June 2). U.S. graduation rate continues decline. *Education Week* [online edition]. Retrieved from www.edweek.org/ew/articles/2010/06/10/34swanson .h29.html

Takeuchi, L. (2011). *Families matter: Designing media for a digital age*. New York, NY: Joan Ganz Cooney Center at Sesame Workshop. Retrieved from http://joan ganzcooneycenter.org/Reports-29.html

Takeuchi, L., & Levine, M. H. (in press). Learning in a digital age: Towards a new ecology of human development. In A. Jordan & D. Romer (Eds.), *Media and the well-being of children and adolescents*. New York, NY: Oxford University Press.

Takeuchi, L., & Stevens, R. (2011). *The new coviewing: Designing for learning through joint media engagement*. New York, NY: Joan Ganz Cooney Center at Sesame Workshop.

Thai, A. M., Lowenstein, D., Ching, D., & Rejeski, D. (2009). *Game changer: Investing in digital play to advance children's learning and health*. New York, NY: Joan Ganz

Cooney Center at Sesame Workshop. Retrieved from http://joanganzcooneycenter. org/Reports-18.html

Toppo, G. (2012, January 31). White House office studies benefits of digital games. *USA Today*. Retrieved from www.usatoday.com/news/washington/story/2012–01–26 /educational-video-games-white-house/52908052/1

Torres, R. J. (2009). *Learning on a 21st century platform: Gamestar Mechanic as a means to game design and systems-thinking skills within a nodal ecology.* Unpublished doctoral dissertation.

U.S. Department of Education. (2012, September 21). *ED Review*. Retrieved from www2.ed.gov/news/newsletters/edreview/2012/0921.html

Woodard, E. H., IV, & Gridina, N. (2000). *Media in the home: The fifth annual survey of parents and children.* Philadelphia, PA: The Annenberg Public Policy Center.

Young, M. F., Slota, S., Cutter, A. B., Jalette, G., Mullin, G., Lai, B., ... Yukhymenko, M. (2012). Our princess is in another castle: A review of trends in serious gaming for education. *Review of Educational Research, 82*(1), 61–89.

MICHAEL H. LEVINE *is founding executive director, Joan Ganz Cooney Center at Sesame Workshop, New York, USA, and can be reached via e-mail at michael.levine@sesame.org.*

SARAH E. VAALA *is the Martin Fishbein postdoctoral fellow at the Annenberg Public Policy Center, University of Pennsylvania, and can be reached via e-mail at svaala@asc.upenn.edu.*

NEW DIRECTIONS FOR CHILD AND ADOLESCENT DEVELOPMENT • DOI: 10.1002/cad

INDEX

OTHER TITLES AVAILABLE IN THE
NEW DIRECTIONS FOR CHILD AND ADOLESCENT DEVELOPMENT SERIES
Reed W. Larson and Lene Arnett Jensen, Editors-in-Chief
William Damon, Founding Editor-in-Chief

For a complete list of back issues, please visit www.josseybass.com/go/ndcad

CAD136 **Independent Child Migration–Insights into Agency, Vulnerability, and Structure**
Aida Orgocka, Christina Clark-Kazak, Editors
This volume contributes to a growing body of literature on international independent child migration. It gives particular focus to agency and vulnerability as central concepts for understanding the diverse experiences of children who have migrated alone. These concepts provide theoretical and empirical insights into the complexity of children's experiences. Combining perspectives from academics and practitioners, the volume challenges readers to critically assess the categorization processes related to both migration and childhood that independent child migrants encounter, and argues for greater attention to the ways in which categories are constructed in theory and practice. Reading this collection will provide scholars and practitioners with thought-provoking insights into the nature of current programmatic interventions for independent child migrants. It further invites researchers, practitioners, and policy-makers to critically reflect on the complex socio-economic, political, and cultural contexts in which migration decisions are taken. Contributors recognize that independent child migrants, despite vulnerabilities, are active decision-makers in determining movement, responding to violent and discriminatory situations, resisting stereotypical assumptions, and figuring out integration and life choices as these are shaped by existing structural opportunities and constraints.
ISBN 978-11183-52823

CAD135 **Family Conflict Among Chinese- and Mexican-Origin Adolescents and Their Parents in the U.S.**
Linda P. Juang, Adriana J. Umaña-Taylor, Editors
Parent–adolescent conflict in immigrant families has long been conceptualized as inevitable due to the inherent stresses of the acculturation process; this volume provides a more nuanced understanding of parent–adolescent conflict in Chinese- and Mexican-origin families in the United States. In their chapters, authors explore key issues related to family conflict such as acculturation gaps, parent and adolescent internal conflicts, conflict resolution, and seeking out confidants for help in coping with conflict. This volume showcases the complexity of conflict among Chinese- and Mexican-origin families and furthers our understanding of how both developmental and cultural sources of parent–adolescent conflict are linked to adjustment.
ISBN 978-11183-09117

CAD134 **Youth Civic Development: Work at the Cutting Edge**
Constance A. Flanagan, Brian D. Christens, Editors
Civic engagement of young people is increasingly understood as an important feature of democratic functioning in communities, organizations, and societies. It has also become clear that the civic domain is indispensable as a context for understanding human development processes. This volume brings together cutting-edge work from leading scholars in the interdisciplinary field of youth civic development. Their work makes the case for greater consideration of justice, social responsibility, critical consciousness, and collective action in our understanding of child and adolescent development.

The volume proposes the following central theses in relation to youth civic development:
• It is rooted in the realities of young people's everyday lives.
• It is collectively constructed.